Gardens
for Birds

Hummingbirds & Butterflies

GARDENS FOR BIRDS,
HUMMINGBIRDS & BUTTERFLIES

Series Concept: Robert J. Dolezal
Encyclopedia Concept: Barbara K. Dolezal
Managing Editor: Victoria Cebalo Irwin
Photography Editor: John M. Rickard
Designer: Jerry Simon
Layout Artist: Barbara K. Dolezal
Photoshop Artist: Gerald A. Bates
Horticulturist: Peggy Henry
Photo Stylist: Peggy Henry
Proofreader: Ken DellaPenta
Index: Alta Indexing Service, El Cerrito, CA

President/CEO: Michael Eleftheriou
Vice President/Editorial: Linda Ball
Vice President/Retail Sales & Marketing: Kevin Haas

Home Improvement/Gardening
Executive Editor: Bryan Trandem
Editorial Director: Jerri Farris
Creative Director: Tim Himsel

Created by: Dolezal & Associates,
in partnership with Creative Publishing international, Inc.,
in cooperation with Black & Decker.
BLACK&DECKER. is a trademark of the Black & Decker
Corporation and is used under license.

Library of Congress
Cataloging-in-Publication Data

(Information on file)

ISBN 1–58923–001–9

PHOTOGRAPHY & ILLUSTRATION

PRINCIPAL PHOTOGRAPHY:

JOHN M. RICKARD: All photographs except where otherwise noted below

OTHER PHOTOGRAPHY AND ILLUSTRATION:

MARGIE BROWN: pg. 114 (top)

TIM BUTLER: pgs. 98 (mid), 99 (bot), 103 (top), 104 (top), 109 (top)

CAB COVAY: pg. 99 (mid)

ROBERT J. DOLEZAL: pgs. 105 (bot)

DOUG DEALEY: pgs. 23 (bot L), 36 (bot), 37 (top R), 80 (mid), 82 top L & bot L)

DAVID GOLDBERG: pgs. 66 (bot), 114 (mid)

SAXON HOLT: pg. 96 (top)

HORTICULTURAL PHOTOGRAPHY: pg. 109 (mid)

DONNA KRISCHAN: pgs. v, viii, 2 (bot), 4 (mid), 5 (bot), 6 (top), 7 (bot), 9 (top), 11, 14 (top), 16 (top R), 19 (bot), 22 (mid), 30, 34 (lower mid L, upper mid R), 62 (bot L & R), 67 (step D), 70, 72, 80 (bot), 111 (bot)

PETER LATOURETTE: pgs. 82 (upper mid)

DON LANGE: pgs 9 (mid & bot), 18 (top), 21 (top), 34 (lower mid R), 78 (bot R)

OTTO MOLTZ: pgs. 5 (mid), 20 (bot)

JERRY PAVIA: pgs 96 (mid & bot), 98 (top), 101 (bot), 108 (top & mid), 109 (bot), 110 (top), 112 (top & bot), 113 (top & bot), 115 (mid)

CHARLES SLAY: pgs 21 (top), 104 (bot), 114 (bot), 115 (bot)

TINA SMITH: pg. 111 (top)

ILLUSTRATIONS: HILDEBRAND DESIGN

ACKNOWLEDGEMENTS

The editors acknowledge with grateful appreciation the contribution to this book of Wild Birds Unlimited, Dublin, CA, and Betsy Niles, Sonoma, CA

Gardens for Birds

Hummingbirds & Butterflies

Author
Linda D. Harris

Photographer
John M. Rickard

Series Concept
Robert J. Dolezal

*Landscaping to welcome
wildlife to your yard*

CREATIVE
PUBLISHING
international

MINNETONKA, MINNESOTA

www.creativepub.com

C O N T E N T S

INTRODUCTION

M y appreciation of plants and birds began early. Both my parents were interested in nature, and they pointed out various birds and plants to me throughout my childhood. Our suburban kitchen window faced the backyard, where Dad's bird feeder was stationed. We often watched birds from this window; it was a kind of shared family pleasure. My first memories of backyard birds are of bright cardinals and brilliant blue jays among the shining, prickly leaves and red berries of the holly tree, and of the comforting sound of mourning doves as they cooed to each other. The first butterflies I recall were the yellow sulphurs and white cabbages I saw during recess in elementary school. The thrill of my first encounter with a hummingbird eluded me until I was almost 40—but it was well worth the wait!

Cedar waxwing feeding on ripened fruit.

> "*I've watched you now a full half-hour;*
> *Self-poised upon that yellow flower*
> *And, little Butterfly indeed*
> *I know not if you sleep or feed.*
> *How motionless!—not frozen seas*
> *More motionless! and then*
> *What joy awaits you, when the breeze*
> *Hath found you out among the trees,*
> *And calls you forth again!*"
>
> WILLIAM WORDSWORTH

Western tiger swallowtail on lilac.

As I found when I was just a little girl, birds and butterflies add to the enjoyment of any garden. When you superimpose another dimension—that of living, moving color—over ground-rooted plants, you add a more intense, more dramatic, and more personal element to your landscape. You will notice that when you purposely attract birds and butterflies to your garden, you immediately increase your awareness of sight and color, sound and fragrance, the seasons, and your own anticipation of change.

Whether your garden already exists or is still in the planning stages, you readily can add elements to draw birds and butterflies. In just a few weeks, your plantings will work their magic. Before you've put down your spade on the last group of flowers you plant, you'll probably have a wildlife visitor nearby. And as time passes and your plantings mature, more and more birds, hummingbirds, and butterflies will fly by and stop in to enjoy the habitat that you've created especially for them.

Wildlife gardens that attract birds, hummingbirds, and butterflies are a great pleasure on many levels. They're a sensual feast, full of color, texture, and fragrance. One of the most appealing aspects is the active element of motion that birds and butterflies bring to the landscape. While trees, shrubs, and flowering plants—however striking they may be—are static, these wild visitors are the extra jewels that catch our attention with their movement. They flit here and there, free and always unpredictable, constantly changing; they're tremendously enjoyable to watch as they weave their colorful lives through our gardens.

As you learn more about birds and butterflies, you'll come to realize they have unseen behaviors and traits that extend beyond their beautiful wings or musical calls. The plants, shrubs, and trees you choose for your garden will transform your landscape into a beacon for many wildlife species.

> Make your garden come alive by inviting winged wildlife to stop by and stay awhile amid the flowers in your landscape

Gardens for Birds and Butterflies

You can enjoy birds and butterflies anywhere around your home: in the flower garden, on the patio or deck, at window feeders, or anywhere else you choose. When you invite wildlife into your landscape, you'll be much richer for the experience. In turn, you'll also make your garden an extension of the native environment that provides your winged visitors a place to rest, food to restore their bodies, and sites to rear their young.

How can you increase enjoyment of birds, hummingbirds, and butterflies in your yard? In the pages that follow, you'll learn the basics about butterflies and many varieties of birds that are common visitors to home gardens. You'll learn to recognize the attractions that they're seeking in your landscape and the many ways you can provide them with food and shelter. You'll also see how these winged visitors can help your gardening efforts by eating pest insects and aiding flowers in their pollination.

Let's start by sharing ideas about adapting your existing landscape to make it more appealing to birds and butterflies.

Your first reaction to seeing this colorful shelter for butterflies might be to wonder, "Narrow sparrows?" Opinion is mixed regarding the benefit that such shelters offer butterflies; add one to your yard for its whimsical and decorative values rather than for practical purposes.

NATURAL HABITATS TO WELCOME WILDLIFE

Birds, hummingbirds, and butterflies may randomly visit any garden, but by planning habitats that draw them, it's easy to increase their number and the frequency of their visits. Once these jewels of moving color discover the delights of your garden, they're likely to return to it again and again.

The requirements of birds and butterflies are simple: reliable sources of food, water, safety, and shelter. Create welcoming environments by choosing and growing plants that are likely to attract them—and by including water features, feeding stations, protection from predators, and privacy. Whether designing an all-new garden or adapting an existing landscape, you can either concentrate your bird and butterfly garden in just one area or include attractive features throughout your yard.

Regardless of the scope of your garden, an environment near fresh water and filled with welcoming plants is sure to attract wildlife. Layered plantings—plants of various heights and differing growth habits—provide visual interest and offer variety in both food and shelter. You can incorporate plants with seed heads, nectar flowers, or berries, or plant vines to cover a wall or post. Try a few large containers of flowers or add a few hanging baskets on a patio. Plant ground covers, both to provide shelter and to harbor the insects on which many birds feed. You can plant a formal foundation, grow a garden of brilliant annual flowers, or plant some fruiting trees and shrubs. Whether tiny, huge, or somewhere in between, the haven you create will entice and welcome wildlife. As you plan and bring your wildlife garden to completion, sure enjoyment is in store.

(Above) Using seed to entice birds to visit your garden is a tried-and-true technique. A boulder serves as a junco's dinner table in this natural setting.

(Right) Butterflies will find a field of open-faced flowers irresistible because of their bright colors, pollen, and nectar. As the flowers fade, seed will form and birds will gather to feast on it.

BUTTERFLIES

Which is it, a question mark or a comma? Is it a monarch or a viceroy? What exactly does a skipper look like? Have you ever been captivated by a polyphemus moth or a spring azure? All these are members of LEPIDOPTERA, the order that includes true butterflies and their close relatives, skippers and moths. Let yourself be charmed by each of them, up close.

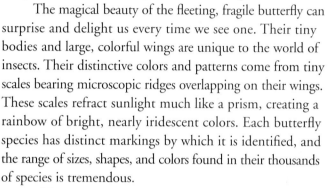

The magical beauty of the fleeting, fragile butterfly can surprise and delight us every time we see one. Their tiny bodies and large, colorful wings are unique to the world of insects. Their distinctive colors and patterns come from tiny scales bearing microscopic ridges overlapping on their wings. These scales refract sunlight much like a prism, creating a rainbow of bright, nearly iridescent colors. Each butterfly species has distinct markings by which it is identified, and the range of sizes, shapes, and colors found in their thousands of species is tremendous.

Although butterfly and moth species vary from region to region, from climate to climate, and from season to season, many can live out all four stages of their lives—from caterpillar to mature winged beauty—in your landscape when you provide them the basics of life. Bright flowers, sheltering trees, host plants to feed their caterpillars, and a sunny place to drink and sunbathe will draw them to your garden for close observation. Be sure to include among your plantings some parsley, yarrow, or other herbs, which are particularly attractive to butterflies.

On a breezy day, butterflies will take shelter in a protected flower garden. Give them some moistened sand and you may host an entire congregation of fluttering drinkers that will spangle your garden. For added enjoyment, identify and record the winged beauties that drop by your yard. Children especially delight in watching this live-action science project. Plan a viewing area—either indoors or a quiet seat outdoors—and you'll have hours of entertainment year after year.

(Top left) Coloration in butterflies serves several purposes. The bright markings of this zebra longwing identify the insect to potential mates while warning predators of its bitter taste. It is resting on an incense cedar branch.

(Inset) The monarch is among the most common butterflies in North America. Its native range extends throughout most of the United States and southern Canada.

(Left) The buckeye, shown here sitting on a yellow coneflower, is another common North American butterfly whose range extends from southeastern Canada throughout much of the U.S. Because they tolerate only mild weather, they migrate to warmer locales when temperatures begin to dip.

GARDENS TO SUSTAIN

Think of your wildlife landscape as a one-stop shop for birds, hummingbirds, and butterflies. Ideally, when they fly in for a drink or a snack, they'll find their other needs are met in your garden and choose to stay there. A landscape that sustains will offer a complete habitat, supporting and protecting all the wildlife living within it. Sustenance of a species within your landscape requires long-season food sources, even year-round supplies. Many birds will come to your yard in search of food; when your landscape contains groupings of summer, autumn, and winter fruits, plus several supplementary feeding stations, these avian visitors can become long-term residents. To draw a wide range of birds, position feeding stations high for wary species, vertically along trunks for perching varieties, and near the ground for birds that browse for their food. Among the most endangered bird species are those that forage on the ground; they are easy prey unless they're provided protection.

Flying visitors also need spots to perch and bathe. Ponds of all sizes, or other water features such as bog gardens or fountains, will attract and keep birds in your yard.

Include some or all of these necessities in your plans, and your habitat will be a haven that draws all sorts of birds and butterflies and encourages them to stay

(Top right) A water feature in your garden will provide more than a drink to your feathered visitors; it's also a place to bathe. This young warbler is taking a rest to allow its feathers to dry.

(Inset) When winter arrives and snow covers the ground, fruiting shrubs such as holly are a source of berries, which are filled with stored sugar and the oily seed that birds require.

(Right) Fruit-bearing trees and shrubs are popular for such birds as waxwings. To provide an even flow of food, plant trees that fruit progressively throughout the season.

HUMMINGBIRDS

It's possible that the first time you encountered a hummingbird, it was the sound you first noticed. Their flight creates a very loud humming sound, hence their name. It's quite startling that such a loud sound comes from such a minute creature.

Despite their small scale, these flying gems are bold, territorial, fearless—even fierce. Male hummingbirds bear brilliant, exotic plumage, a result of the way light hits the surface of their feathers rather than any specific color pigment they contain. Females bear more muted coloration that better suits their lives spent in nest building and provides them camouflage for egg sitting and baby rearing.

Hummingbirds use enormous amounts of energy because of their high metabolism and strong, fast flight. They eat spiders and small insects—which they sometimes catch midair—stopping frequently to drink lots of fresh water and nectar. They need safe spots to perch, rest, and observe their surroundings. In addition, they require a dry, protected perch on a tree branch or beneath an overhang where they can shelter from rain. As you read more in later chapters about how to attract them, you'll discover ways your garden can include a suitable habitat for hummingbirds [see Attracting Hummingbirds, pg. 74].

(Top left) Their fast metabolism— rate of energy use—requires each hummingbird to constantly search for food. Plants such as butterfly bush are lush with flowers filled with nectar and pollen, and they attract small insects the birds eat.

(Inset) Close observation of your hummingbirds in spring and early summer likely will lead you to their diminutive nests. This black-chinned hummingbird has a nest filled with tiny eggs.

(Left) Red, deep-throated flowers will draw hummingbirds to your garden. The tiny birds are very territorial and will return to the planting over and over again. An immature ruby-throated hummingbird takes a sip of nectar.

GARDENS TO SHELTER

Birds and butterflies are well suited to life outdoors. Still, they seek shelter in various forms throughout the year. There are a variety of plantings and garden features to consider when you want to attract birds or butterflies to your premises.

Examine your yard. It should comprise an overstory of trees with high foliage in a few areas; a midstory of shrubs, bushes, and tall flowering plants beneath the trees, along fences, and in borders; and an understory of grass, ground cover, and low-growing flowering annuals and perennials. Your garden also may offer areas of full sun, partial shade, and shade, allowing you to grow many different plant species. If some of these habitat zones are missing from your garden, you may add them by installing new features that are designed to attract wildlife [see Habitat Planning, pg. 34].

(Right) Birdhouses are subsitutes for hollows in trees and nesting spots in rock niches that visiting birds will appreciate. Remember that some species also nest on the ground, in burrows, in hanging locations, or atop posts.

(Below) Keep tall shrubs and trees a distance away from birdbaths and ground feeders to keep bird predators from hiding in them and using them for cover.

Encourage birds to linger in your landscape by offering them perches for nesting and hiding, and plan to include areas for ground browsing that are safe from predators. A single large evergreen tree—a fir or cedar, for example—a trio of lilacs, or a grouping of hollies can afford birds these advantages. Leave faded perennial plant stalks in the garden over winter to provide loose nesting material, and install nesting boxes and birdhouses to shelter birds—not just for a day or two but to encourage them to stay—where they're protected from household pets and away from foot traffic and in children's play areas. Garden structures such as shade arbors, pergolas, arches, and trellises are usually well visited by birds and sometimes support a nest or two.

Dense shrubs and hedges, especially evergreen species, are excellent bird shelters, offering protection from extreme cold weather and the strong winds that commonly accompany the onset of winter. Winter-hibernating butterflies will shelter in protected tree hollows or cluster under foliage. Even a dead tree—if it's located at a safe distance from your home or paths—is an asset, providing refuges from inclement weather, food sources, and perching spots for migratory birds.

Besides furnishing shelter, offer a constant and ample supply of food and water. The wildlife in your garden will come to count on it as a supplement to natural fare.

SONGBIRDS

What fun it is to anticipate the return of birds after a long winter and to watch them raise their young. Indeed, it's the very image of spring! While winter birds, with their colorful plumage and interesting behaviors, are a joy to watch, songbirds, with their melodic calls, are a special treat in the home landscape. Once your garden offers exciting places to nest, eat, and drink, you'll soon enjoy a host of bird visitors and be able to observe them in their various life stages and activities.

(Top left) White-crowned sparrow is one of several sparrow species with similar appearance and overlapping ranges from the arctic to Mexico.

(Below) Provide perches in your wildlife garden with plants or by adding roosting poles, woven-wire cables, or other high and safe spots. They may be visited by a female dark-eyed junco such as the one shown here.

(Bottom) A male eastern bluebird is brightly colored; the feathers of its mate are mostly gray.

Each songbird's call is unique to the species. After you have had opportunities to observe the birds and hear their songs, you'll learn to recognize their calls. Cardinals, chickadees, mockingbirds, robins, warblers, and wrens all have easily identifiable songs. Also, songbirds bear distinctive markings, but it sometimes takes the sharp eye of an experienced bird-watcher to identify the often subtly colored females of certain species.

To attract songbirds, your garden must include food plants to which they're particularly drawn. Some smaller bird species like thistle seed; plant some—or let some grow naturally, as the case may be—for the avian harvesters to enjoy. Other songbirds enjoy the seeds of coneflower, cosmos, and sunflower. Sow some of these plants for birds to harvest naturally as their flowers fade.

You also can supplement food supplies by setting up bird feeders. If you particularly want to attract smaller birds, cover feeders with a cage of hardware cloth. Suet, hung out in mesh bags or spread into bark crevices in a hanging log, is a good winter attractant for carnivorous birds. Change it frequently as the weather begins to warm, then discontinue it after trees sprout leaves and flower.

Songbirds also will feast on berries and fruit, especially blueberries, cherries, mulberries, and the bramble fruits. Thorny canes make safe perching spots, while medium to large shrubs and small trees offer suitable perching and nesting areas. Many small birds such as purple finches and wrens choose to build their nests in hanging baskets—breeding pairs sometimes return to the same nest year after year—so hang out a few baskets for everyone to enjoy.

WATER GARDENS

Water is a magnet to wildlife. If you have a stream on your property, you probably already have a huge variety of wildlife visiting year-round. Even a simple birdbath on the lawn, however, can draw a wide selection of birds for facinating close-up viewing. If the water makes a splashing sound, it will be even more attractive—thoroughly irresistible, to many species of wildlife.

Providing water in your landscape can be easy and simply accomplished or elaborate in planning and design. Consider including a pond, fountain, waterfall, bog garden, half-barrel water garden, or small pool, depending on the scale of your landscape. Any of these can make a lovely focal point in your garden while beckoning to birds. You can include watercourses, falls, or sound-producing effects; they'll require more effort to plan and install than will simple, self-contained fountains or ponds. Floating plants or fish will add another dimension while attracting frogs and turtles. Use natural-looking rocks, copy wildlife settings, and include foliage overhangs to shade the water, creating habitats and crevices in which water creatures can hide. Other animals may come to drink and live near water, and your pond may develop its own tiny ecology.

Ponds containing fish sometimes also attract fishing birds—heron, egret, and kingfisher—as well as neighborhood pets. Any of these can deplete a pond of its ornamental fish in a matter of hours, so provide cover in the form of floating lily pads and overhanging foliage that helps keep them safe.

Regardless of whether your pond is a home for fish, it's essential to remember that garden water features pose a hazard to young children and some pets. Always keep them safe by erecting fencing around the feature and providing plant barriers, bridge railings, and constant supervision.

(Inset) Water features of any scale will draw birds to your yard. They need little more than fresh water in a shallow basin with room to perch.

(Right) Where space permits, a garden pond and stream with running water will serve a large population of birds. If you add a shallow beach, butterflies will rest and drink, too.

Many other interesting birds besides hummingbirds and songbirds will come to your garden once you incorporate plantings and features to attract and shelter them. Seek out the best means of enticing birds of all kinds, sizes, and colors.

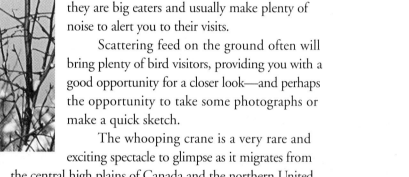

OTHER COLORFUL BIRDS

WINTER VISITORS

When it's winter outside, watch birds from the comfort of your home. You'll be sure to see them if you provide them food and water. Offer supplemental food and a heated fountain or birdbath to keep them coming.

Count on the cardinals, doves, eagles, game birds, hawks, owls, sparrows, starlings, waxwings, some woodpeckers, or other year-round residents of your area. As winter gives way to spring, you'll see some new migrating birds visiting your landscape.

Record the species you see. Involve your children, starting them on a lifetime hobby. The birds will thank you by visiting, and that's the only reward you'll need.

You may see or hear small downy or hairy woodpeckers if you have a wooded area nearby; they'll hang around if you offer suet for feeding through the winter. Flickers, hawks, mourning doves, owls, plovers, pheasants, and quail might wander in to grace your landscape in their normal range of activity, but they'll return regularly if you have provided food and water for other birds. Jays and magpies are always a cheerful spectacle; they are big eaters and usually make plenty of noise to alert you to their visits.

Scattering feed on the ground often will bring plenty of bird visitors, providing you with a good opportunity for a closer look—and perhaps the opportunity to take some photographs or make a quick sketch.

The whooping crane is a very rare and exciting spectacle to glimpse as it migrates from the central high plains of Canada and the northern United States to the Gulf coast; other common cranes, egrets, herons, and storks are more frequently seen. Noisy, interesting characters such as cowbirds and grackles will also visit, usually in sizable flocks, eating whatever is available and tasty, then moving on.

Freshwater birds such as Canada geese, mallards, and many ducks are interesting to watch if your garden includes a large water feature to support their presence. Some travel in large flocks—they are quite a sight, flying in formation—while others stick close as pairs. Salt marsh birds and shorebirds such as cormorants, flamingos, herring gulls, ibis, pelicans, sandpipers, and spoonbills are welcome in coastal gardens. All exhibit interesting behavior when found in their preferred habitats. As some of these birds migrate, you'll find yourself first missing them, then looking forward to their next annual visit.

Ground-foraging game birds such as these California quail have distinctive markings and an endearing plume. While common in wildland fields, they frequently visit suburban homes that border their range.

BLOOMS TO ATTRACT

Providing flowers is one of the easiest ways to quickly entice winged wildlife to your garden, but what flowers are most attractive?

Flowering plants call to wildlife in ways other than through their appearance—our human notion of beauty. For instance, a flower laden with eggs, larvae, or beetles may feed a hungry carnivorous bird; a flower that's past its prime—going to seed—will attract the attention of many seed-feeding species.

One reason to plant alder, birch, maple, and poplar trees is for their catkins and seed, which appear early in the year before perennials and annuals have gone to seed. Wrens and other colorful small birds will cover the branches of these trees in midspring as they busily pick seed from the trees.

Colors, scents, and shapes all entice birds and butterflies to visit flowers, which offer nectar, places to land, and feasts of insects, seeds, or berries. For instance, daisies provide a flat landing surface and feed zone for butterflies. Clustered, nectar-bearing flowers attract them to alight, drink, and lay their eggs. Sweet-scented flowers such as petunias and sweet William draw butterflies to drink their nectar. Tubular and tightly clustered flowers such as lilac and columbine attract hummingbirds. Deep-throated flowers with nectar such as honeysuckle and nasturtium entice butterflies, hummingbirds, and orioles, while frequently hosting insects that serve as food for insectivores. A flock of hungry grazing birds may help keep insect infestations from becoming established and aid the gardener in maintaining an environmental balance that will discourage infestation and disease.

When birds feed from plants, they aid in plant propagation in two ways: by helping spread pollen, and by passing seed through their digestive systems. Many plant species actually depend on winged visitors for propagation. You'll soon find that all of nature interacts within the garden, to the benefit of all the animal and plant species found there.

A natural garden with a mix of trees, shrubs, and flowering plants is ideal for birds, hummingbirds, and butterflies. Choose plants for their ability to produce flowers, fruit, nectar, and seed throughout the season.

A nyone of any age can enjoy gardening for wildlife. If you like to watch birds and butterflies, make the move beyond a basic home landscape of a turfgrass lawn and a few bordering shrubs. You can expand into the symbiosis of nature's plant and animal kingdoms, discovering the interconnections that match wildlife populations with environment and habitat. Right there, near your own window or in your outdoor living space, you really can get close to the nearby natural world. Birds and butterflies, as well as many other interesting forms of wildlife, will soon come within easy observation range. Many probably already do!

When you are ready to purposely invite birds, hummingbirds, and butterflies to visit your surroundings, you'll first have to consider a few options. If your site is sunny and protected, butterflies and hummingbirds will be a natural choice on which to focus and to attract for a closer view. Large, shaded areas are perfect for many beautiful bird species. It's also a good idea to consider fencing if you have household pets in your neighborhood since a well protected area is more likely to encourage birds to return.

> Flowering plants, trees, and shrubs offer birds and butterflies the two things they need most—food and shelter

Welcoming Wildlife to Your Yard

As you get started gardening for wildlife, you can work with your existing plant material, enhancing it by saving some plantings while adding more, or by starting over from scratch. In this chapter, you'll find more specifics about butterflies, hummingbirds, songbirds, and other birds, and then you'll learn about different types of plants—trees, shrubs, berries and fruit, vines, and ground covers—to incorporate in your landscape as purposeful attractants. You'll also find information about plant sources and helpful resources, in addition to facts about tools, equipment, and plant health to help you plan your wildlife habitat. By careful selection, you'll fill your garden with plant species that offer a range of food and shelter, protection and nesting places, perching spots, and nest-building materials. You will put out the welcome mat for the birds and butterflies that will come by your garden month by month, season by season, and all year round, thrilling you with their beauty.

A wildlife garden for birds and butterflies should contain food, host, and shelter plants. It also should have quiet areas, ample barriers to provide protection from pets and predators, a source of water, and plants at ground level, midheight, and overhead.

BUTTERFLIES

The silent, fluttering charm of butterflies among your garden plants is a sure thing when you grow flowering plants in a sunny place. Add a water feature or a shallow puddle, and there you have it—a butterfly paradise. Even the most frequently observed varieties—white cabbage butterflies, hairstreaks, monarchs, mourning cloaks, painted ladies, sulphurs, and swallowtails—are a delight. Look for extraordinary moths, such as the luna, remarkable for its giant size, coloration, grace, and beauty. The startlingly large polyphemus moth can measure up to 5½ inches (14 cm) across. Its equally amazing larva looks like a round, green concertina with tufts of hair all over it. Even bigger is the cecropia moth, reaching as wide as 6¼ inches (16 cm). Its caterpillar is huge, green, and stubbly.

Regardless of its remarkable beauty, every butterfly and moth was once a lowly, wormlike caterpillar. A butterfly goes through vast changes during its four-stage life cycle. From an insignificant egg, one of many deposited together on leaves or stems by the female adult, a hungry caterpillar—or larva—hatches. The caterpillar stages of some butterflies and moths are quite unusual, colorful, distinctive, or just plain interesting. Hatching from eggs laid on carefully chosen plants, the caterpiller begins feeding on the host plant. It grows, shedding its skin several times. It eats more and more of the host plant, sometimes requiring a crawl-over to another host plant. The larva keeps eating until it reaches a mysterious stopping point triggered by chemical changes within. Then it begins one of the most interesting periods, the pupal—or resting—stage. After anchoring itself somewhere suitable—a twig or small branch, for instance—it slowly hardens into a chrysalis. Within that alien form, the caterpillar's cells respond to powerful chemical hormones, reforming the larva into a beautiful winged adult that emerges to live, mate, lay eggs, until it finally flutters to the earth for the last time.

(Insets) Even the larva of a monarch butterfly is distinctive (above). Its appearance remarkably differs from the woolly bear caterpillar (right).

(Right) Bush lantana, seen here, and its close relative, trailing lantana, both have long-lasting blooms that continue from late spring until the first frosts. Their bright-colored flowers are favorites for many species of butterfly.

All butterflies and moths have specific preferred plant hosts for their larvae. Each adult seeks out its own unique plant species upon which to lay its eggs. Monarchs, for example, are called "milkweed butterflies" because their existence is irrevocably linked to that plant family. Some adult butterfly species feed from nectar flowers during their lifespan, which may be as short as just a few days or as long as a few months. Others ignore food sources and focus their brief adult lives on mating, finding their host plant, and laying their eggs.

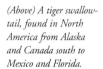

Male adult butterflies and moths fly irregularly because they are tracing scent patterns from the females—called "pheromones"—carried on wind currents. Butterflies land on bright flowers that match their mates' coloration patterns, sometimes with no idea of feeding; you can attract certain varieties by planting flowers colored like the females of their species. If adults are to persist in your garden, they will need brightly colored nectar flowers, including butterfly bush, butterfly weed, clover, and daisies of all kinds, to mention just a few. Plant those annual and perennial flowers and shrub foliage plants in your garden that will provide needed host plants for the butterflies' eggs.

Butterflies will return to flowers that offer the best location and food for their offspring. If your garden is hospitable, many butterfly species will deposit their eggs in it to create future generations. With their variety in size, wing markings, and colors, and their fragile yet unerring flights and landings, butterflies will charm you, your children, and your neighbors, and leave you wishing for more encounters. Invite them into your garden with the flowers and features they are seeking.

(Above) A tiger swallowtail, found in North America from Alaska and Canada south to Mexico and Florida.

(Left) Those with small-space gardens still can host butterflies; plant your butterfly flowers in containers for a deck.

(Inset) Butterflies use tall flowers as perches upon which to rest, as well as sources of food.

(Left) A butterfly garden can be beautiful and still serve its purpose. The red, pink, and white valerian seen here has abundant, fragrant, clustered flowers that attract butterflies. When the blooms fade, they form seed for birds.

HUMMINGBIRDS

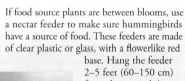

Adorable or awesome? It's hard to decide! Sound and a fury of blurred wings are the first signs of a hummingbird in your garden. The rapid wing beats cause the characteristic humming sound, which is really quite loud and startling the first time you hear it. Brilliant, iridescent plumage glows in the sunlight, drawing your eye. For small creatures, typically 3½–5 inches (90–125 mm) long, they're not shy.

Hummingbirds are so tiny, yet so energetic that they need large quantities of food—about half their weight every day—to provide enough calories for their metabolism. All during their hyperactive day, hummingbirds feed. With their long beaks, they reach deeply into tubular flowers, and extend their long tongues to drink while hovering precisely in front of the flower they've chosen. Before long, the tiny bird is off somewhere else, almost quicker than your eye can follow, diving, then ascending straight up, sometimes even flying backward.

The various species of North American hummingbirds are rather separated by locale. Only the ruby-throated hummingbird is found in the eastern United States and Canada, though there sometimes are rare sightings of a wayward rufous or Cuban emerald. In the west, there are at least 17 hummingbird species in a variety of ranges. The species are especially varied in the southwestern desert areas of the United States, Mexico, and into Central America. Hummingbirds migrate hundreds—even thousands—of miles. How such tiny birds with so little body fat can travel so far—twice a year— remains a subject for curious wonder.

The males and females migrate separately. At his return to his breeding area in spring, a male stakes out his territory with an eye to a mate. He fiercely defends his home area, from courtship through mating. Then he moves on, while the female stays and does the nest construction, incubation, and rearing of the minuscule young.

To attract hummingbirds, be sure to include a variety of their favorite plants in your landscape. Large deciduous trees and shrubs with bright flowers—red flowers in particular— are preferred by hummingbirds. Consider planting a trumpet creeper, which they'll find irresistible. Choose from among red buckeye, butterfly bush, fuchsia, red trumpet honey-suckle, lilac, penstemon, flowering quince, flowering sage, and weigela, which also will please them.

FEEDERS

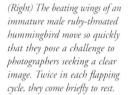

If food source plants are between blooms, use a nectar feeder to make sure hummingbirds have a source of food. These feeders are made of clear plastic or glass, with a flowerlike red base. Hang the feeder 2–5 feet (60–150 cm) from the ground, in a protected, sunny spot. Powdered nectar mixes are available, or you can make your own from table sugar and water [see Artificial Nectar, pg. 75]. Keep the feeder filled and fresh. After hummingbirds discover it, you'll be refilling it several times a week!

(Right) The beating wings of an immature male ruby-throated hummingbird move so quickly that they pose a challenge to photographers seeking a clear image. Twice in each flapping cycle, they come briefly to rest.

(Below) Layer your butterfly garden with brightly colored flowers of many different species. Pick those plants with wide, flat faces, clustered blooms, or with nectar-filled flowers.

Hearing birdsong is one of those ethereal experiences that transcend and reward you. Cardinals, chickadees, finches, mockingbirds, and wrens all have lovely songs and will sing them to you freely if you welcome them to your garden.

SONGBIRDS

"Songbird" is a commonly used classification without any scientific standing, a group that includes many different types of birds. Birds in this category often have brightly colored plumage and have beautiful songs or other endearing qualities—quickness, boldness, odd ways of flying, and so forth—giving each species a distinct personality and charm that is especially treasured.

Virtually all birds "sing" to some degree. Their songs fall on human ears much differently than on those of another bird. We love their musical lilt and apparent abandon. But what that birdsong says in its pitch, duration, and construction is quite specific to the birds found in its area. Females may hear the siren call of a suitor; males may hear a warning from another bird with a territory to defend; a sentry may voice concern about a passing predator; a mother may call to her chicks.

Songbirds are carnivorous, herbivorous, or omnivorous, depending on the species. Providing each with its specialized diet can add balance to your garden landscape. Some songbirds are ground dwellers or ground foragers, hunting for grubs, insects, worms, and fallen seed. Others, including flicker, robin, sparrow, and thrasher, burrow into the ground in search of grubs and worms. Some birds eat seed and berries from atop stalks or limbs—the finch, waxwing, and wren are good examples—while others such as jay, mockingbird, and thrush eat insects from perches on foliage. Shrike and thrasher pry insects from crevices; grosbeak, mockingbird, and nuthatch crush and crack nuts and hard-shelled seed; and flycatcher, martin, and swallow are specialized hunters that hunt and eat insects on the fly.

Because of all these varied bird species, their preferences for eating, and their differences in diet, your wildlife landscape should offer a wide selection of plants to entice and satisfy every charming songster.

(Left) This flock of house finches quickly can empty a feeder of its seed. Check yours and refill it often.

(Above) A mated pair of mountain bluebirds strip aphids and seed from wild anise, or licorice.

(Below) Fledgling wrens soon will develop their adult coats.

OTHER BIRDS

More than 500 species of birds inhabit the world of today. Beyond songbirds and hummingbirds are others that are valuable additions to the garden. Some of these other species may be so-called accidentals, or casual visitors, while others are residents.

Look for the muted gray of doves, colorful wood ducks, kingfishers, quail, roadrunners, swifts, or tanagers in their varied habitats. Keep an eye out for nuthatches and woodpeckers; they'll come for suet. Mourning doves and game birds—grouse, partridges, pheasants, and quail among them—are all ground feeders that love grain.

If you live in a wooded area, you'll see raptors such as eagles, falcons, hawks, and kites. Owls prefer the same habitat; the great horned owl mates in winter and calls hauntingly through the snowy woods.

In coastal areas, ospreys are a treat to view. There also are a host of water and wading birds—freshwater lake, salt marsh, and seashore.

(Right) Mourning doves are a common sight in many suburban and rural areas. Their three-part cooing is distinctive, as is the drumlike sound they make when they take flight.

(Below) Look for downy woodpeckers on the trunks of decaying trees and standing snags. Their sharp, pointed bill penetrates deep into crevices in the wood to find burrowing insects.

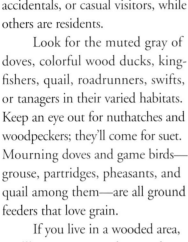

You'll likely find that attracting some of these birds to your garden may discourage others. Some species—cowbirds, jays, and mockingbirds—are brash, robbing food, laying their eggs in the nests of other birds, or emptying bird feeders in record time. Choose birdhouses with small entry holes and wrap seed stations with hardware cloth that allows small species to enter but excludes nuisance birds. In a complete . and balanced ecology, however, all species have their place.

Flowering plants make lovely plantings while also drawing birds and butterflies. The varied heights and growth habits of these plants match the habits of birds, making them ideal for mixing throughout landscapes of shrubs and trees. For example, tall sunflowers grow seed heads in autumn that are easily reached by birds perched in nearby trees. Cosmos, of medium height, produces seed heads suited to birds that perch in woody shrubs and low evergreens. Low-growing plants, including wild strawberry, are good feed for ground foragers.

FLOWERING PLANTS

NECTAR-PRODUCING FLOWERS

While people usually are interested mostly in a plant's flower color or shape, butterflies and hummingbirds are drawn to their nectar and fragrance. In the process of feeding, they rub against the stamens and pistils of the flowers and help aid pollination. Bleeding heart, cardinal flower, trumpet creeper, fuchsia, *Hemerocallis flava*, honeysuckle, and salvia (perennial, annual, and herb species) all are irresistible to hummingbirds. Tubular florets hold nectar at just the right angle for gathering by hummingbirds and pollinating insects, including butterflies. Aster (perennial and annual), buddleia, catnip, honeysuckle, lilac, peppermint, phlox (perennial and annual), sedum (particularly *S. spectabile*), spearmint, sweet William, verbena (annual and perennial), and zinnia are all good choices. Remember also that flat-faced flowers—mostly daisies—provide good perches for butterflies at rest.

For best results, choose a selection of plants and set them in your garden in groups of five or more. Many colorful perennials and easy-to-grow annuals are attractive to birds, hummingbirds, and butterflies. Flower scent, shape, and color all contribute to the attractive powers of plants while providing pleasing results to your landscape design. Consider these for your wildlife garden:

Annuals and Biennials: Alyssum, calendula, centaurea, cosmos, dahlia, dianthus, heliotrope, *Hesperis matronalis*, honesty, lantana, marigold, mignonette, nasturtium, pentas, petunia, phlox, salvia, scabiosa, snapdragon, stock, tithonia, verbena, vinca, and zinnia. Hesperis, honesty, and mignonette will grow in shade.

Perennials: Achillea, *Alyssum saxatile*, anaphalis, *Anemone* x *hybrida*, arabis, asclepias (*A. incarnata*, *A. speciosa*, *A. syriaca*, and *A. tuberosa*), aster, aubrieta, *Baptisia australis*, bidens, *Centranthus ruber*, *Cimicifuga racemosa*, cirsium, columbine, coreopsis, *Dictamnus albus*, erigeron, goldenrod, hemerocallis, hibiscus, hollyhock, lavender, liatris, loosestrife, lupine, monarda, penstemon, phlox (*P. divaricata*, *P. maculata*, *P. paniculata*, *P. pilosa*, *P. stolonifera*, and *P. subulata*), purple coneflower, rudbeckia, santolina, scabiosa, *Sedum spectabile*, *Spiraea latifolia*, and turtlehead. Anemone, centranthus, cimicifuga, columbine, hemerocallis, and the phloxes will grow in shade.

Wildflowers: Boneset, clover, dandelion, dock, evening primrose, Joe-Pye weed, mallow, nettle, plantain, Queen-Anne's-lace, and thistle. Plant these in full sun.

Vegetables: Corn, carrot, parsley, and sunflower. Plant in full sun.

Herbs: Angelica, anise, basil, borage, chives, dill, fennel, hyssop, sweet marjoram, mint, oregano, rosemary, sorrel, and thyme. Plant most in full sun; angelica and sorrel will take some shade.

The breast feathers of many species of warbler are tinged with golden yellow. Immature birds such as the one seen here may be difficult to identify. Seed eaters, they search out plants such as this wild mint.

TREES

Both large deciduous shade trees and their counterpart evergreen trees provide shelter, nesting areas, perching safety, and even the small territories required by most bird species during nesting times. Some butterfly species may use tree hollows or leaves for hibernating. Large trees also may provide food by hosting insect populations, which normally inhabit the bark or leaves, and by bearing berries, flowers, fruit, or nuts.

Some excellent trees to consider for attracting birds are southern or eastern red cedar, box elder, fir, sweet gum, hemlock, holly, oak, pine, spruce, western sycamore, and black gum tupelo. These handsome trees need plenty of time and space to develop their mature size and spread. They are long-lived, valuable additions to any home landscape. Small trees with fruit such as birch, crabapple, dogwood, hawthorn, holly, juniper, redbud, shadbush, sumac, and willow also will draw birds; they'll enhance your property as well. Fruit-bearing trees—standard or dwarf—such as apple, apricot, cherry, peach, pear, persimmon, plum, and quince can contribute to the bird menu. Hungry birds will quickly pick a fruit tree clean.

Before you select trees, match their needs to your light conditions. Choose several large trees and a larger number of small trees for an attractive balance in the landscape. It's important to select trees that are well suited to your region. For a guide, use the United States Department of Agriculture (USDA) Plant Hardiness Zone maps, divided into 11 climate regions based on their shared average lowest winter temperatures and duration of cold [see Plant Hardiness Around the World, pg. 116]. Pick your trees by checking their labels for plant hardiness information (usually expressed as a numeric range, such as "Hardy in Zones 7–9"); avoid selecting tree species bordering on the edge of your hardiness range.

Lesser goldfinch (top), white-crowned sparrow (middle), and pair of juvenile ruby-throated hummingbirds (bottom).

SHRUBS

Birds make use of shrubs for camouflage and safety, for food, perching, and nesting, while butterflies hibernate or lay their eggs on them. These woody plants come in a wide range of sizes and habits. Take advantage of this great variety; select at least three different species—more, if you have space—and plant them in groups. For example, choose several taller species such as viburnum, then group medium-height shrubs such as azaleas to form understory plantings. Groups of three to five plants of the same shrub species are best for making a pleasing arrangement.

Barberry, shrub roses, and other thorny shrubs with densely matted, spiny or sharp-pointed branches make great protected spots for perching and nesting. Evergreen shrubs help wildlife by offering privacy and a buffer against winter wind. Shrubs also may offer berries, fruit, or nuts, as well as supply insects for food sources. In severe weather, hedges and densely branched shrubs provide shelter from falling rain and snow. Birds perch among shrubs with the intention of keeping an eye on the ground and nearby open spaces, for browsing and for early notice of predators.

Many deciduous shrubs will draw wildlife as well. Select varieties with bird- or butterfly-attracting features that spread over several seasons, and include those with autumn fruits to ensure a banquet that lasts. For spring bloom and nectar, good choices are fragrant azaleas (usually deciduous types), bridal-wreath, lilac, rhododendron, viburnum, and weigela. For summer bloom and nectar, choose from butterfly bush, honeysuckle, mock orange, roses, and wax myrtle. Highbush cranberry, euonymus, hackberry, nandina, and pyracantha are good fruit providers. Many evergreen shrubs are irresistible, including azalea, bearberry, blue-berry, juniper, rhododendron, yew, viburnum, and small to medium-sized varieties of holly such as the popular winterberry.

As you do for trees, match your shrubs to your landscape's light conditions before you acquire plants. Many shrubs prefer light shade, but some need full sun to fruit well. When you plant shrubs, be sure to allow for their mature height and spread so the plants can have adequate room for their future growth.

(Left) Mourning doves feed on the catkins of shrub willow in springtime in many areas.

(Below) Butterfly bush is an aptly named shrub with colorful blooms that compete for beauty with its fluttering winged visitors, here a swallowtail butterfly.

BERRIES AND FRUIT

Fruiting plants provide good feed as they bear their crops, offering shelter and nesting sites throughout the rest of the year. Birds will nest where there is sure to be food, so your fruiting plants encourage them to choose your garden as the spot to raise their young. Between fruit crops, the trees and shrubs also shelter the birds from rain.

(Top) Many flowering fruit trees, like this cherry, become magnets to flocks of birds when their fruit begins to ripen.

(Bottom) Another avian favorite is drying plums. All species of fruit trees are good choices to plant in a garden to attract birds.

As you consider plants, keep in mind that early-flowering species bear fruit the earliest, while those that bloom later in the season will bear their fruit in autumn. Some fruiting plants have berries that persist into winter. By choosing and mixing several species with staggered bloom and fruiting times, you'll provide the birds with a steady food supply. About half of your selected shrub species should be those that bear berries, fruit, or nuts. For the most attractive arrangements, select at least three different species, and plant them in clusters of three to five plants. Also create natural thickets that birds can use for safe nesting; thorny fruiting plants such as barberry, pyracantha, and raspberry are excellent choices.

Other valuable plants to consider are bayberry, blackberry and other bramble fruits (dewberry, black raspberry), dogwood, elderberry, hazelnut, holly, mulberry, pokeberry, serviceberry, shadbush, and viburnum. If you already grow any of the luscious table berries such as blueberries, raspberries, or strawberries, you know how much the birds like them, too. Birds will feed on apples, apricots, cherries, crabapples, nectarines, peaches, pears, plums, and quinces, either the cultivated or wild species, knowing instinctively to start eating at the moment the fruit becomes ripe. If you want to save some berries and fruit to eat yourself, protect a few branches by covering them with bird-proof netting soon after the green fruit forms, and pick it soon after it ripens.

Most fruit-bearing plants need full sun for best bloom and good production. Protect them from wind in exposed sites and and stake vining plants or tie them to support wires. Plant shade-loving perennials or ground covers such as bunchberry or yew beneath your fruit trees to attract ground-browsing birds. Space your plants at least the recommended distance to allow sun to penetrate, to maintain good air flow, and to provide for easy care and cleanup. In low sites with more sun, plant alpine or mock strawberry as ground cover; they both bear small, edible fruit filled with seeds.

WINTER FEED

Many small trees and shrubs bearing berries, fruit, and nuts, as well as perennial and annual flowers that hold seedpods, help provide good eating to avian visitors during the cold winter. Ornamental grasses, if left unsheared, are also plentiful seed sources. Persistent berries such as dogwood and holly are particularly valuable when snow covers the ground. In cold-winter climates, plants such as these will be picked clean before spring. In cold weather, in order to maintain their body heat and energy, birds require at least as many calories as they do when temperatures are moderate. Supplement natural winter food with bird feeders [see Winter Feeding Needs, pg. 82].

GRASSES, VINES, AND GROUND COVERS

When selecting vines, grasses, and ground covers for your wildlife landscape, consider plants that have a long flowering or fruiting season, or those that bear bright flowers, seed, or nectar. Before making your final selections, check each plant's light and soil requirements, plant hardiness zone, and care needs to be sure it will perform will in your garden. For plants that attract butterflies or hummingbirds, choose a planting site where they will feel protected but you'll still be able to view them up close.

Grasses: Consider including ornamental seed-bearing grasses in your garden. Many perennial landscaping grasses that form large, bunchlike clumps such as andropogon, miscanthus, and pennisetum also provide food, shelter, and nest-building materials for birds. Avoid sterile varieties—those that flower but lack seed.

Vines: By planting vines, you'll satisfy the needs of many winged visitors. Songbirds choose vines for nesting and shelter; hummingbirds visit red-flowered types, especially trumpet creeper and honeysuckle; and butterflies enjoy those that bear tube-shaped blooms with nectar. Include in your landscape plans some English ivy (especially the smaller-leaved types), climbing hydrangea (*H. petiolaris*), Virginia creeper (*Parthenocissus quinquefolia* and *P. cuspidata*), and wisteria to grow up posts and trail over fences.

Many vines will grow easily on masonry or wood walls. Protect your structures by building a support of hardware cloth over a wood frame that stands 2 inches (50 mm) out from the wall and is anchored to it at top and bottom. Other vines may perform better with some training, tying, or fastening to a support. For these, what could be more appropriate than an arbor? For sturdy, strong arbors, try clematis (especially *C. montana*), grape, greenbrier (*Smilax* species), passionflower (*Passiflora* species), climbing rose (included here even though it lacks the clinging tendrils of true vines and requires support), trumpet creeper, and wisteria. For trellises and lightweight supports, plant asarina, cardinal vine, cypress vine, glory vine, red-flowered varieties of honeysuckle (especially choice is *Lonicera* 'Alabama Crimson'), hop vine, hyacinth bean, moonflower, climbing nasturtium, scarlet runner bean, rhodochiton, or climbing sweet pea.

Ground Covers: Some vines make great ground covers, quickly filling in areas after planting. Vines such as English ivy, Virginia creeper, and other low plants are excellent when used for larger areas in full sun. You might also consider clover; lowbush cranberry; spreading phlox (*P. stolonifera* and *P. subulata*); cultivated, mock, and wild strawberry; moss verbena; and vetch. For the shade areas of your landscape, consider leadwort, *Vinca minor*, and violet—this last flowering ground cover will provide nectar for your wildlife visitors as well as dainty color and pleasing aroma for you. Deciduous ferns do well in moist-soil areas, while providing nest-building materials and dense shelter.

(Top) Wherever stands of grass and cattail rise above boggy soil, look for yellow-headed blackbirds harvesting seed and building their carefully disguised nests.

(Bottom)Keep ground-foraging birds in mind such as this white-crowned sparrow. They hop through grass and ground cover in search of nutritious seed and insects.

GARDEN CARE

When you're growing garden plants for birds and butterflies, it's especially important to use organic gardening practices and consider overall environmental health. Because of the interconnectedness of garden species, control agents used for weeds, insects, or diseases will have direct effect on your flying visitors. It's best to start with natural controls, such as hand picking, releasing beneficial insects, and washing with plain water.

If you do apply pesticide to control an infestation of one insect, several things are sure to happen. A Japanese beetle with spray residue on it, for example, may be eaten by a bird before or after the insecticide takes effect but before it dissipates or degrades. Its active ingredients then become a part of the bird's tissues. Should a crow then eat that bird, the chemicals again are transferred to the predator's body. If your pet catches the crow, the cycle continues within the pet's body. With each step, the pesticide becomes more concentrated and likely to cause hazard. And back in your landscape, each successive generation of insects that receives a dose of insecticide tends to have some individuals that survive and reproduce, passing along a genetic resistance to the control you've used. Over time, the application of pesticides may lead to long-term, detrimental effects. It concentrates pesticides and garden chemicals in the food chain and reduces numbers of beneficial predator insects, while creating control-resistant pests.

Instead, your aim should be the natural balance of a complete environment, allowing small populations of various insect species—pests, beneficials, and others—in the soil, in the air, on branches, bark, and leaves, at all seasons of the year. Birds will feed on the insects they find, helping to keep their populations in check.

Grow your plants using normal healthy garden practices: watering, mulching, fertilizing, and pruning. Inspect your plants once a week to see if any pests or diseases have arrived or developed. Hand pick insects or wash them away with a strong stream of water. If you see disease, manage it by pruning off any infected plant parts and providing more air circulation. Always destroy diseased prunings and disinfect your shears to prevent spreading the disease to other plants in your garden.

(Top) Resist the temptation to deadhead fading flowers if you wish for birds in your garden.

(Middle) Loosely trimmed hedges have many interior branches that birds will find ideal for nesting.

(Bottom) Vining flowers such as morning glory require support. Tie their tendrils loosely with stretchy plant tape to a lattice.

This type of care is very practical, more economical, and easier because it involves you in the ecology of your landscape. By selecting healthy plants, you will reduce the likelihood of regular infestations. Do recognize that natural controls will allow a relatively small population of weed and pest organisms to persist as the price paid for a balanced environment.

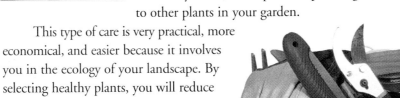

CHOOSING HEALTHY PLANTS

Plants that are healthy are in a state of normal, active growth and function. It's a continuous condition that begins when a plant is very young—seedling, cutting, or division—and continues throughout the plant's life to maturity if it receives even

supplies of water and nutrients, the correct light intensity, room for roots and branches to grow and expand, and time to mature. Repeated interference with any of these basic needs will affect the plant's growth and performance.

It's important to know the quality of the nursery or garden center where you will acquire plants. Is it clean and neat? Are plants healthy and well-tended? Carefully examine any plants you're considering by inspecting roots, stems, and leaves for signs of damage, insects, or disease. Choose sturdy, compact plants without wounds on stems or branches. Check to make sure the main growth top—the leader—has not been pruned or broken off. Look for vigorous, full growth and attractive green foliage—or, since some plants are colored or variegated, color typical of the species and variety. Look under leaves and along stems and branches where many signs of insects such as egg clusters may otherwise go unnoticed. Avoid obtaining plants that show evidence of infestation by any of these pests:

(Left) Start your garden off right by choosing plants that visiting birds, hummingbirds, and butterflies find attractive and picking healthy specimens.

(Below) Ask your garden center about the right plants for your climate, region, and special soil conditions. Avoid crowding your plantings, using only the number required to achieve the spacing recommended for each species.

Aphids—translucent, in various sizes.
Spider mites—fine webbing across leaves, with a dusty, stippled, or faded look.
Whiteflies—fly up in clouds when plants are moved.
Scale—small, rounded, brown or gray, shiny bumps on woody trunks, stems, or the undersides of the leaves.

Pass over any infested or stunted plants. Select species that are most resistant to regular heavy infestations of pests or diseases to avoid future infestations; you can find this information in most plant encyclopedias [see Encyclopedia of Popular Bird and Butterfly Plants, pg. 95]. Choose plants nurtured by organic growers who are known to avoid the use of pesticides—such plants frequently bear organic identification tags. Plants obtained from large garden centers usually are in best condition shortly after their arrival. Those shipped from growers to direct retailers normally are pest-free and healthy since they must meet stringent certification regulations at the time of shipment.

Growing your own plants from seed is a good way to make certain that healthy organic practices are followed all the way through their lives. Barring that, check to see if your supplier provides a guarantee, including replacement if the plants should fail to grow.

CHOOSING TOOLS AND EQUIPMENT

If you've been gardening for a period of time, you probably have most of the tools you'll need for your bird and butterfly plantings. Basic planting equipment include a hoe, a rake, a step-on shovel or spade, and a leaf rake. Opt for good quality tools; if well cared for, they'll last a lifetime of gardening. Some tips: look for stainless steel heads that have tangs—metal extensions—going down into the handle where they are firmly bolted. You can select tools with light aluminum or fiberglass handles and comfortable grips, or smoothly finished wooden handles made of ash or oak. Those with rubber or foam grips make handling easier, too.

A pair of high-quality, comfortable pruning shears is another essential. You'll use them for deadheading, cutting off broken twigs and branches, cutting flowers for bouquets, and thinning plant stems. Before you choose, try them while wearing your preferred garden gloves to find shears that fit your hand and whose size and weight are appropriate to your hand size and strength.

Heavy leather or heavy fabric garden gloves with a waterproof coating give your hands the most protection and will give good service. Next, you'll need a watering can and garden hose. Select a heavy-duty watering can that will hold at least 1 gallon (3.8 l) of water and has a comfortable handle; if it has a diffusing rose—or sprinkling head—so much the better. Look for a garden hose of at least ⅝-inch (16-mm) diameter; it will provide water volume more quickly than do smaller-diameter hoses. You'll need a hose holder, too, to keep the hose out of the way of mowing or foot traffic.

A garden cart or wheelbarrow will be extremely useful if your planting area is large. Consider a cold frame, too, if you live in a cold-winter climate with a short gardening season and you want to raise any perennials or annuals from seed. And you'll need a dry, clean place to store your tools between gardening forays. Maintain your fine tools by cleaning them after use, lubricating their working parts, promptly sharpening cutting edges, and keeping them at the ready for the next project.

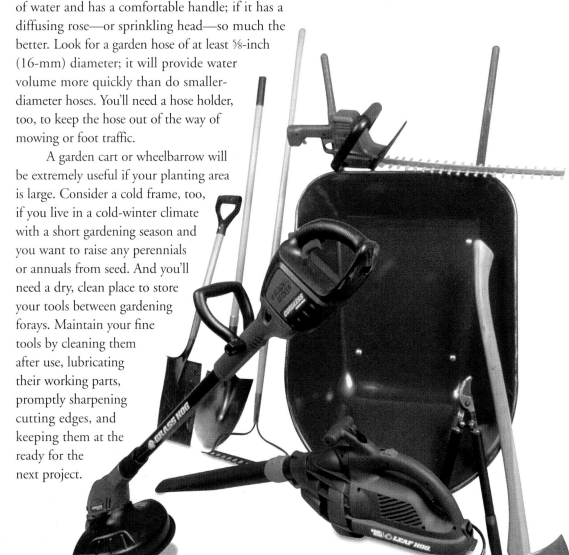

A wildlife garden is easier to care for when you have the right tools: (clockwise from top) an electric hedge trimmer, wheelbarrow, axe, lopping shears, leaf blower, string trimmer, shovel, spade, and garden rake.

SOURCES AND RESOURCES

Near your own backyard—or close by, anyway—are the best places to acquire plants as well as gain the benefit of valuable experience. Local nurseries and retail garden centers usually stock plants that are well adapted to your region, and their staffs should be familiar with your area's soil and climate as well as the plants that thrive there. They also will be able to coach you on each plant's specific needs. Garden club sales are another good source of plants; you'll sometimes find wonderful, even rare, plant varieties to cherish. Botanical gardens also sponsor plant sales and are a good source of information on local native plant species.

Farther afield, you'll find brief cultural descriptions in plant and seed catalogs from direct merchants. These retailers are usually excellent sources of plants. Look for companies that state a generous guarantee, at least through one growing season. Prices for good-sized, ready-to-bloom plants from direct merchants may be higher than at some local sources, but keep in mind that the quality and selection are excellent. Many direct merchants have a presence in the electronic marketplace; find them by checking their ads in periodicals or by searching electronic information resources.

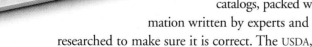

At some point, you may wish you had someone more experienced at your elbow to help you decide about choosing or placing a plant, or to help identify a visiting bird or butterfly. Excellent advice is yours for the asking from local gardening and bird-watching clubs, and from gardening neighbors and friends. You'll find a wide range of books and other printed materials at your local garden store. Also, bookstores and libraries usually stock basic gardening texts and field guides, and there's a regular crop of quality gardening periodicals and catalogs, packed with well-researched information written by experts and researched to make sure it is correct. The USDA, Agriculture Canada, or university cooperative extension in your area is another reliable source. Many extension offices have information available on attracting butterflies and wildlife; some use trained volunteer Master Gardeners to assist or advise home gardeners. A search of electronic information sources will also yield much useful information [see On-Line Index, pg. 118].

(Above) Seldom is it so simple to tell the plant a butterfly would choose as is shown in the nursery here, where a variegated fritillary paused for a moment on the plant identification tag for its host, garden verbena.

(Left) Use electronic resources to help you find useful information on plants and wildlife.

(Below) Seed and plant catalogs, periodicals, and other direct merchant literature are good sources for many landscape plants.

PLANNING FLOWCHART

A flowchart is a planning tool that allows you to scan the important questions that need to be answered as you plan your garden. In landscaping, as in most other projects, there is a sequence in which tasks should be done. By planning an orderly flow of tasks and arranging for tools and materials to be on site when needed, you can reduce wasted time and duplicated effort. As you go through the following questions you can also develop the timetable for your project.

GARDENS FOR BIRDS

1 Are you primarily interested in attracting birds? Are there any species that particularly interest you? Do these species have certain diet and nesting habits or specific shelter requirements? Which plants would best serve the bird population you wish to attract? Have you started your plant list? Will you include a water feature? Will you add feeding stations and birdhouses as part of your garden design? From what perspective will you view your garden? Will birds feel safe in your garden and be protected from household pets and other predators?

GARDENS FOR HUMMINGBIRDS

2 Are you primarily interested in attracting hummingbirds? What flowering plants and other plants will fit their specific feeding requirements? Will your garden incorporate plants that will provide safe perching spots and nesting sites? Have you started a plant list? Will you include a water feature? Will you include a few nectar feeders as a part of your garden design? Will you incorporate window boxes and hanging plants? From what perspective will you be viewing your garden? Will hummingbirds feel safe in your garden?

GARDENS FOR BUTTERFLIES

3 Are you primarily interested in attracting butterflies? Are there any particular species of interest to you? Do these species have certain diet and life habits or specific shelter requirements? Will each butterfly species find host plants on which to lay its eggs? Do you have a sunny area for your butterfly garden? Which plants would best serve the butterfly population you wish to attract? What flower colors would you prefer? Have you started a plant list? Will you include a water feature? From what perspective will you view your garden? Will butterflies be able to visit your garden in safety?

4 What is the extent of your garden? How many features will you include? Where will they be situated? Will you sketch out a garden plan or seek the help of a landscape designer? How will the garden enhance the style of your home? Will you incorporate structures into your garden? What are the soil and drainage conditions, and do they need to be improved? Will you include new utilities (water, electricity), features (pond, fountain), or maintenance systems (irrigation)? How much time are you able to spend on maintenance? Have you allowed adequate time to plan and install the project? What is your budget?

PROJECT PLANNING AND GARDEN SYSTEMS

CHOOSING PLANTS

5 Have you observed other gardens and made notes about plants you'd like to include in your own? Have you started your list of desirable plants? Which plants best suit your garden situation (sun, shade, soil)? Have you checked each plant's spacing based on its mature size and habit? Will you include large trees? Do your plans include plants to provide shade, shelter, fruit, nectar, seasonal flowering, long blooming periods? What aquatic plants and fish will you need for your water feature, if any? Where will you acquire plants? Does the supplier provide any guarantee? Where will you obtain garden and maintenance supplies? What is your plant budget?

GARDEN INSTALLATION

6 Will you install your landscape or will you seek professional aid? If you require other aid, do you know of a good source? When do you expect your garden plan to be completed? What are the size and place-ment of permanent structures (pond, fountain, deck, patio)? How long is needed to erect or install each feature? Will you install everything at once or in phases? How long will each phase take to complete? Have you acquired the tools, equipment, and materials necessary for the first phase? Where will you find sources of information and advice? Are there specialists or retailer staff —or libraries, extension offices, public gardens, arboretums— who can offer advice?

Make choices,
plan a habitat,
and design your
plantings—the
keys to having
a great wildlife
garden

A garden that attracts wildlife can be formal or informal, wooded or sunny, colorful or green. It may contain trees and shrubs, or perhaps just flowers. You've already seen some natural habitats and have begun to form some ideas for your own bird, hummingbird, or butterfly garden [see Chapter One: Gardens for Birds and Butterflies]. You also may have visited public gardens, botanical preserves, and arboretums—either in person or through the pages of periodicals or electronically via television or an electronic resource. Now it's time to begin designing your garden.

The information on the following pages will help you create your own personal haven for wildlife. You'll begin by performing an evaluation of your site, taking into consideration the light it receives and its protection from wind and rain, its soil type and condition, and drainage issues. Next, you'll sketch your ideas for plantings that will attract birds and butterflies. All the while, you'll ponder whether to add garden features such as fountains and birdbaths or other elements necessary for garden care such as walkways and irrigation systems. You can even include structures for your personal enjoyment such as gazebos, decks, and patios. You'll see, step-by-step, how to draw a garden plan, build a post-mounted birdhouse, and plan utilities for a water feature.

Creating Gardens for Wildlife

You'll discover when to amend your soil to meet the needs of plants you want to grow, and when it's best for them to grow in native soil. Finally, you'll begin to design your plantings—for that purpose, we've included a list of plants commonly grown for winged wildlife—and decide on ways to protect the birds and butterflies that are sure to visit.

You're free to create something unique and beautiful, to enhance your home and your own garden and wildlife interests, with boundaries found only in your imagination. You can install your garden all at once or stage its construction and planting over time. It's completely up to you. Enjoy!

Essentials for any bird garden include the right flowering plants, shrubs, and trees; weatherproof feeding stations with easy access; low-voltage lighting for safety; and a rain gauge to accurately measure precipitation and help you decide when to irrigate.

SITE ANALYSIS

Before designing your bird, hummingbird, or butterfly garden, examine your site carefully with wildlife in mind. Note its slope, drainage, and natural water sources; the direction of prevailing winds; the type of terrain, plus any large rocks or special soil conditions; the position of existing trees and shrubs; the area's particular climate fluctuations; and light and shadow movement during the day.

Light exposure is especially important. Observe the sunlight's movement, identifying areas with light throughout most of the day, those chiefly in shade, and those between these two extremes. Note that light patterns will shift somewhat as the seasons turn.

As you examine your site, consider those elements already in place. If there are large rocks, will you keep or remove them? Perhaps you'll bring large boulders to the site. Also, decide if any of your existing plants will remain.

Before planning your plantings, identify your USDA Plant Hardiness Zone. Every plant hardiness zone is a generalized reference based on the average lowest winter temperature. It's important to know your zone so the plants you choose will adapt well and thrive in your garden [see Plant Hardiness Around the World, pg. 116]. Experienced local gardeners, garden center or nursery staff, and local university, USDA, or Agriculture Canada extensions can provide zone recommendations.

Each plant species grows best in certain climate conditions; beyond their native habitat's temperature extremes they seldom are hardy. But because microclimates—localized climatic variations—occur quite frequently, it's possible for a banana plant, for example, to live through most winters in a zone that's colder than its native tropical habitat. Microclimates are affected by several factors: land elevation, airflow, wind protection or wind prevalence, presence of open water, moisture conditions, and soil type, among others. As you might expect, microclimates can change as buildings or trees are removed or added.

Finally, evaluate your yard from various viewing perspectives. Think about your garden's appearance from the street, porches, patios, decks, and balconies. Also consider the view from various windows in your home, so you will be able to enjoy your garden and its wildlife visitors, even while indoors.

Helpful tools to use for evaluating your garden include a weatherproof thermometer (above), a magnetic compass (upper right), and a rain gauge (right inset).

(Right) This sloped hillside filled with flowers previously was a grassy knoll. The owner recognized its potential as a butterfly garden.

(Inset) A sundial reminds us to check the location of sun and shadows several times each day.

CREATING A GARDEN PLAN A garden plan—often called a base plan—is a scale diagram of your bird, hummingbird, or butterfly garden. Two steps must be taken for an accurate plan to result: careful measurement of the yard, and transfer of the measurements to paper or a computer equipped with design software. If you choose to automate the process, follow the instructions of the software producer for best results. Here, the traditional process is used, following these steps:

1 Using a tape measure, stakes, and string, note the size of the outside perimeter of your plan's area. Note the center point and radius of each curve.

2 Using two fixed points, such as corners of the area, measure the distance to each structure or existing garden element.

3 Mark on the plan the exact locations of all electric or water fixtures, along with any trees, shrubs, or other greenery that you plan to keep in your landscape or garden.

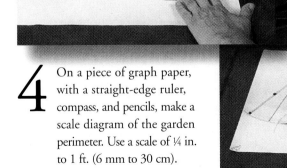

4 On a piece of graph paper, with a straight-edge ruler, compass, and pencils, make a scale diagram of the garden perimeter. Use a scale of ¼ in. to 1 ft. (6 mm to 30 cm).

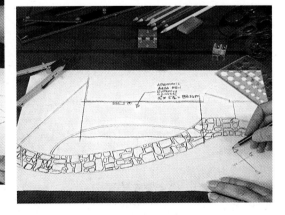

5 Using a compass, measure arcs at the locations of structures, garden elements, utility access points, and plants.

6 Complete your garden plan by noting North and each of the other cardinal directions in the margins of the diagram.

HABITAT PLANNING

A complete habitat consists of areas that supply reliable and appropriate food, ample water, shelter, nesting, and safety from predators and pets. As you plan your garden, keep in mind the specific species and varieties of birds, hummingbirds, and butterflies you seek to attract to the site. You may want to include several different types of areas in your garden to attract a variety of wildlife.

First, consider including some sort of a water feature in your habitat, so birds and butterflies will be apt to stay for a drink, a bath, or a meal. Water is essential to all types of visitors and will lure many of them to your garden. While large water features will require piped water and electrical power that should be installed before your other garden elements, they can be as simple as a birdbath or a self-contained fountain [see Planning Water Features, pg. 40].

Perhaps you will want a garden of vivid annuals or the carefree ease of flowering perennials to provide color, attract wild birds and butterflies, or produce pollen, seed, and nectar for your visitors' diet. Always remember to include aromatic herb gardens for full-sun areas.

Birds, hummingbirds, and butterflies may be willing to feed, drink, and bathe rather close to your home if their surroundings provide privacy, protection from predators, and shelter from wind, noise, and activity. Add areas for feeders, if desired, installing them where they will be easy for you to maintain and replenish. Plan to include one or several large trees in your garden for perching, or you can install post-mounted birdhouses for tree-nesting birds and hidden boxes at their base to attract ground-nesting species.

Consider planting another area with various seed- and fruit-producing or nectar-bearing flowering shrubs for birds, hummingbirds, or butterflies that feast on their bounty. Such shrubs also will provide safe nesting and perching spots. Familiarize yourself with the mature height and spread of the plants you're considering and allow sufficient space when planting [see Encyclopedia of Popular Bird and Butterfly Plants, pg. 95].

Your habitat also can include winding paths, in-ground irrigation, raised planting mounds, hedges, fencing, walls, and unobtrusive areas for viewing the birds, hummingbirds, and butterflies that will visit. Draw a rough sketch of your ideas, using a bird's-eye view and allowing for the mature growth and spread of plants, then refine your plan [see Designing Wildlife Gardens, next pg.].

Consider nature's answers as you plan your wildlife garden. Will you install feeders for hummingbirds or grow their favorite flowers (top left)? Will your landscape have shelters for butterflies such as this copper, either beneath the greenery or in a butterfly house (above)? Where will birds nest (top right), and where will they bathe (lower right)?

DESIGNING WILDLIFE GARDENS

Designing gardens that will provide food and shelter for birds and butterflies can be accomplished quickly once your garden plan is finished [see Creating a Garden Plan, pg. 33]. Gather colored pencils, tracing paper, a ruler, and eraser, then follow these easy steps:

1 Secure a tracing paper overlay on your garden plan. On separate paper, note some of the features that you want your garden to include.

2 Think first of functions. Use a light pencil to draw circles of various sizes, allocating areas in the garden to their functions.

3 Choose one of the areas as a main feature. Here, a butterfly garden is the central element. Add another tracing paper overlay and sketch ideas of its boundaries and elements.

4 Add an overlay of structural elements and systems, including irrigation lines, power outlets, paths, and observation points.

5 As you complete each area, add it to the overlay. New ideas may require change. Continue until the entire area diagram is complete.

6 Use color shading to identify plant groups. Keep taller plants to the centers of beds or backs of borders, with shorter plants in the margins.

STRUCTURES AND FEATURES

Consider some permanent components as you plan your garden, as related to the habits and behaviors of the wildlife you'd like to see visiting it. Water features are strong attractants for birds, hummingbirds, and butterflies—perhaps a shallow, quiet pool atop a shelf of rock where birds can bathe in full sight, a sand beach for butterflies

(Above) Once birds have become accustomed to your quiet presence, they will accept you and approach nearby. Install a bench for seating in your garden to watch them.

(Right) Chipping sparrows roost on a sturdy chain-link barrier fence that encircles a place of refuge filled with food plants, feeders, and birdbaths. Such a fence will keep animal predators and household pets from entering.

to visit, or a bed of fine sand for bird dusting. Food and shelter, of course, are major draws for birds—include a few strategically placed birdhouses and feeders, as well as hanging posts [see Building a Post-Mounted Birdhouse, pg. 38].

Include structures of a practical nature—sheds, for instance—or accents such as trellises and fencing that will enhance the overall design. Permanent structures that will likely be focal points in your landscape or utilities such as water and electric lines should be placed before plants are installed.

Think about how your wildlife garden will look when observed from your home's windows and from those of neighbors. Choose building materials that blend into the site such as native rock instead of brick. In some cases, the choice is more than a design consideration—pathways of sand and pea gravel, for instance, can be important to certain birds: they ingest the grit to grind their food.

When it's time to install your landscape, place your permanent features while there is still plenty of room to work and you still can avoid harming your plants. If you will be installing structures or walls, begin with the tasks of digging and laying foundations. For water features or lighting, install wiring for power needs and water-supply pipes. The plants that you've chosen will go in last, and then the wildlife will come.

When offering a refuge to wild birds, hummingbirds, and butterflies, remember that they naturally are wary of people and pets. To them, safety means an area that's quiet, has little vehicular or foot traffic, is distant from areas of children's play, and is free of sudden loud noises or moving objects. They also need protection from predators and shelter from the elements. Among the natural enemies of birds are animals that instinctively hunt, including household pets and feral animals. Add a bell to your pets' collars to warn wildlife of their presence, keep your pets indoors, or put them on a lead during peak wildlife visiting hours. Always avoid leaving pets outdoors at night; they may hunt rare native wildlife species, may stray, or may become prey themselves to a larger predator.

Most birds are cautious about nesting or foraging in locations low to the ground where they lack a clear sight of pets and wild predators such as coyote, fox, hawk, raccoon, rodent, and snapping turtle. Safe perching and nesting areas are usually located at least 6 feet (1.8 m) off the ground in trees, post birdhouses, or high atop shade structures constructed for the purpose. Such areas should be placed behind disguised fencing, protected by thorny shrubs such as barberry, bougainvillea, hawthorn, pyracantha, or rose, or surrounded by climb-proof barriers to make them safe for birds. Tree trunks can be encircled by wire mesh barriers to prevent climbing from below.

Birds are also vulnerable to predator attack while bathing, dusting, and feeding. Situate birdbaths and dusting areas in an open area so birds can spot approaching hazards. Place feeding stations far enough off the ground to prevent predator assaults. Some bird species, however, chiefly perch and forage on the ground. Their feeding areas should be situated behind protective wire-mesh fencing or in a large open location that provides a clear view of all approaches. Protect the food source of small birds from larger species by placing their feeders within a cage of mesh hardware cloth with cells large enough for the small birds to easily pass through, yet small enough to bar the passage of larger birds. If squirrels should become a nuisance, some bird lovers provide a separate feeding station for them or use weight-control feeders that can be effective in preventing squirrels and large birds from raiding the food supply.

Wildlife also seek protection from high winds, blowing rain, and snow in foliage and behind windbreaks. Many shrubs and hedge plants with dense branching habits—barberry, holly, privet, and yew are but a few examples—provide excellent sheltered perching during inclement weather. The interior branches of sheared evergreen hedges generally will remain snow free, providing shelter. Solid fencing materials also can provide wind protection. Natural hollows and boxes placed in limb crotches, even in dead trees, will offer safe haven to many birds and over-wintering butterflies. Consider adding them to your landscape trees or fenceposts.

(Left) A post-mounted birdhouse featuring a wide base with a bottom molding that overhangs is an effective barrier for climbing pets or wild animals that prey on birds. They can be obtained at garden centers or built and installed [see Building a Post-Mounted Birdhouse, next pg.].

(Bottom) Protect wildlife from your outdoor pets by attaching a bell to their collars; it's safest for birds and pets alike to keep your household pets indoors.

BUILDING A POST-MOUNTED BIRDHOUSE

This droll mansion will house a flock of wrens, martins, or other small songbirds while adding charm and appeal to your garden. It's assembled in 8 hours from copper flashing, molding, pine, plywood, and dowels using a drill, carpentry and shot-filled hammers, a rotary hand saw, a table saw, sheet metal shears, a socket wrench, and a steel straightedge plus brads, finishing nails, paint, and primer. Gather your materials and gloves, and follow these steps to build the birdhouse:

Required Materials:

Wood Parts:
(see detailed component diagram)

4	Hex Frames
6	Beveled Side Panels
6	Roof Sheathing Panels
3	Baffles
6	Rafter Braces
4	Rafters
6	Copper Roof Flashing Shingles
6	Decorative Molding Sections
12	2-in. (50-mm) Half-Round Moldings
12	4–in (10-cm) Half-Round Moldings
6	⅝-in. (16–mm) Dowel Perches

Other Components:

1	4x4 (89x89-mm) Mounting Fixture
4	Bolts, Nuts, and Washers

Fasteners:

100	6d Galvanized Finishing Nails
25	4d Galvanized Brads

Adhesives and Finishings:

1	6-oz. (175 ml) Wood Glue	
2	Applicator Tubes Panel Adhesive	
1	Qt. (1 l)	Primer and Paint
1	Pt. (0.5 l)	Trim Paint

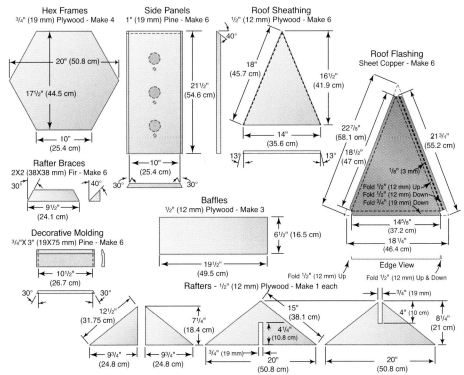

Hex Frames
³/₄" (19 mm) Plywood - Make 4
20" (50.8 cm)
17¹/₂" (44.5 cm)
10" (25.4 cm)

Side Panels
1" (19 mm) Pine - Make 6
21¹/₂" (54.6 cm)
10" (25.4 cm)

40°

Roof Sheathing
¹/₂" (12 mm) Plywood - Make 6
18" (45.7 cm)
16¹/₂" (41.9 cm)
14" (35.6 cm)
13° 13°

Roof Flashing
Sheet Copper - Make 6
22⁷/₈" (58.1 cm)
21³/₄" (55.2 cm)
18¹/₂" (47 cm)
¹/₈" (3 mm)
Fold ¹/₂" (12 mm) Up
Fold ¹/₂" (12 mm) Down
Fold ³/₄" (19 mm) Down
14⁵/₈" (37.2 cm)
18¹/₄" (46.4 cm)
Edge View
Fold ¹/₂" (12 mm) Up
Fold ¹/₂" (12 mm) Up & Down
³/₄" (19 mm)
4" (10 cm)
8¹/₄" (21 cm)

Rafter Braces
2X2 (38X38 mm) Fir - Make 6
30° 40° 30° 30°
9¹/₂" (24.1 cm)

Baffles
¹/₂" (12 mm) Plywood - Make 3
6¹/₂" (16.5 cm)
19¹/₂" (49.5 cm)

Decorative Molding
³/₄"X 3" (19X75 mm) Pine - Make 6
10¹/₂" (26.7 cm)
30° 30°

Rafters - ¹/₂" (12 mm) Plywood - Make 1 each
12¹/₂" (31.75 cm)
7¹/₄" (18.4 cm)
15" (38.1 cm)
4¹/₄" (10.8 cm)
9³/₄" (24.8 cm)
9³/₄" (24.8 cm)
³/₄" (19 mm)
20" (50.8 cm)
20" (50.8 cm)

1 Refer to the parts diagram. Carefully mark and cut each piece to dimension, noting all beveled edges and angles.

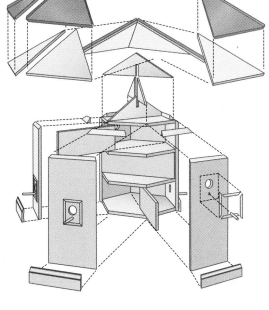

2 Assemble rafters on one of the hex frames, then fit the rafter braces as spacers. Fasten with finishing nails and wood glue.

3 Align the side panels to three equally spaced hex frames, drill holes, and fasten with glue and nails.

4 With three side panels in place, fit the baffles in place to divide each floor in half.

5 Center the post-mounting fixture, and fasten it to the base hex panel using a socket wrench to tighten the nuts to bolts and washers until snug.

6 Add remaining side panels, align top rafter assembly, and fasten it with finishing nails.

7 Align the roof sheathing panels on the rafter assembly, drill pilot holes, and fasten them with finishing nails.

8 Wearing gloves and using metal shears, a shot-weighted hammer, a metal straightedge, and clamps, cut the roof flashing panels and turn their edges to make overlap joints.

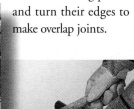

9 Apply water-proof panel adhesive to the roof, fit each roof flashing panel into place, and clamp until dry. Bend each flashing panel's bottom edge and fit it under the roof eaves.

10 Finish the birdhouse by framing with half-round moldings. Add dowel perches, then decorative molding at the base. Prime, paint, and trim.

PLANNING WATER FEATURES

All creatures need water to live, and a reliable source of fresh water will draw wildlife to your garden. As you start to design your water feature, take the following items into consideration to ensure you have the proper scope, site, and resources.

(Above) Two goldfinches visit a birdbath. Keep the water fresh in birdbaths through frequent changes, or install a small pump to circulate and aerate the water.

(Right) While natural appearing, this lovely brook with its water-falls and pools is man-made. It comprises an electric recirculating pump, piping, and a stone-filled watercourse lined with EPDM, a tire-tube-like rubber liner.

First, decide the scope of your project. Will you create an elaborate pond with a waterfall, or install a simple bird-bath? Much depends on your site's size, time available for installation and ongoing care, and your resources.

Is your site in a quiet spot? Is it readily visible? Make the water feature easily accessible to wildlife, and provide for easy viewing. Be sure it fits your space and the scale of your landscape. Evaluate the light conditions, the slope, and the water source. Keep in mind that ponds beneath broad-leaved trees or conifers will collect debris, so they should be located on the upwind side of such trees to reduce care. Include some natural elements in the surroundings—fieldstones, rough wood, and plants—to make the feature more inviting.

Next, consider resources required for the feature's equipment, materials, installation, and ongoing care. With the exception of a simple birdbath, all water features require a recirculating pump plugged into a weatherproof electrical receptacle, with a ground fault circuit interruper (GFCI). Plan for installation of water pipes and power to the site, which may include obtaining a permit from local governmental agencies or the approval of neighbors [see Planning Utilities for a Garden Pond, next pg.].

The professional staff at garden and hardware retailers, adult education programs, and university extensions are all reliable sources of information about water features. They can help you determine pump and piping sizes, choose between preformed and flexible liners, pick finishing materials, and select aquatic plants or fish. Follow their advice when choosing materials and equipment for your project.

PLANNING UTILITIES FOR A GARDEN POND

Power and water are necessary for most recirculating garden ponds. You'll need a GFCI-protected 115-volt A.C. circuit, and either an extension of an existing line or an added circuit. You should plan to lay PVC water pipe to the site from an existing outdoor faucet. All electrical and plumbing work requires care in planning and compliance with building codes; a permit may be required. Prepare for your permit application by gathering your garden plan, drafting tape, tracing paper, a ruler, and pencils, then follow these steps:

1 Make a photocopy of your garden plan, then fasten it to a work surface with drafting tape. Secure tracing paper over it before beginning your drawing.

2 Carefully draw the perimeter of the future pond, locating it precisely and using exact measurements to scale.

3 Mark a boundary outside of the pond, spaced 3 ft. (90 cm) from it. Most electrical codes require that wiring be located at least 30 in. (75 cm) from water features.

4 Route the path of direct-burial electrical wiring or conduit in straight runs, avoiding existing structures, trees, and paving.

5 Route your water supply line in a separate trench. Always maintain a separation distance from the electrical line at least 30 in. (75 cm) wide.

6 Refer to the equipment labels for pumps, lighting, and other equipment. Allow a 25 percent reserve in wattage, voltage, and amperage for your future power needs on the circuit.

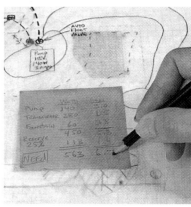

ANALYZING GARDEN SOIL

Soil is important to gardening success; it's essential to your landscape plantings and your yard's health. There are four significant aspects to soil: texture and composition; macro-, micro- and trace nutrients; acid-alkaline balance (pH); and the amount of organic matter—humus—to host living organisms. The best soil is dense enough to hold your plants securely and retain water, yet porous enough to let water and air percolate slowly through it.

Examine your soil by squeezing a handful together, then opening your palm. If the ball quickly falls apart, it's either too sandy or very dry. Soil that clumps together is either mostly heavy clay or very wet. Improve either by adding organic matter in the form of well-rotted manure, humus, or organic compost. Apply a layer 4 inches (10 cm) deep to new beds, then work it in with a tiller or shovel to a depth of 10–12 inches (25–30 cm).

Home soil test kits are available at garden retailers. They measure amounts of nitrogen, phosphorus, and potassium in your soil using chemical reagents. Some kits also measure your soil's acid-alkaline balance, or pH. While the kits generally are reliable, another economical option is testing by a soil laboratory. You can obtain a recommendation for one from your agents at your local university, USDA, or Agriculture Canada extension offices.

Home soil test kits to measure nutrients are available at garden centers and nurseries, or you can send samples to a soil laboratory recommended by your garden center's staff or a university, USDA, or Agriculture Canada extension. Dig several trowel-sized specimens of soil from several different locations throughout the planting area, each at a depth of about 6 inches (15 cm). Mix the samples thoroughly and extract a combined sample for testing [see Soil Testing, next pg.].

Another aspect of soil is its acid-alkaline balance—called pH—measured on a point scale that ranges from extremely acid to neutral at 7.0, then increases to higher degrees of alkalinity. Soil pH affects the uptake of water and nutrients by your plants. A majority of garden soils measure between 5.0–7.5 pH; the best plant soils are 6.0–7.0 pH.

Adjusting pH is easy, but as the amendments are neutralized over time, your soil likely will need repeat treatments. Add garden lime to increase pH; add garden sulfur to lower pH. Read carefully and follow completely the manufacturer's package instructions, including all cautionary warnings, whenever you apply garden chemicals.

PERCOLATION & SOIL TEXTURE

Soil comprises a combination of rock, sand, silt, or clay particles, plus humus, water, and air in the spaces between soil particles. Soil with too much clay drains slowly due to its fewer pore spaces; sandy soils have numerous large pores, and water quickly runs through them. Water generally follows gravity until it reaches a barrier and pools. Keep such pooling water well below the level of plant roots to prevent it from suffocating your plants.

Test percolation by digging a hole 18 in. (45 cm) deep and filling it with water. Water should be absorbed at least 1 inch (25 mm) per hour. If it drains in an hour or less or more slowly, the texture should be corrected by adding organic matter.

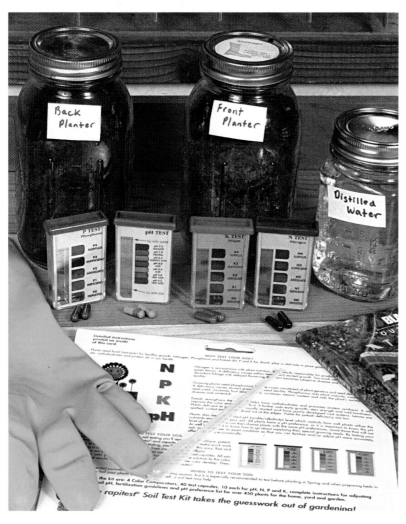

SOIL TESTING

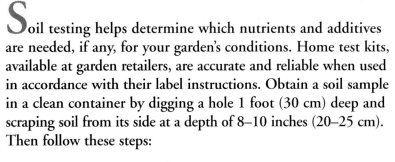

Soil testing helps determine which nutrients and additives are needed, if any, for your garden's conditions. Home test kits, available at garden retailers, are accurate and reliable when used in accordance with their label instructions. Obtain a soil sample in a clean container by digging a hole 1 foot (30 cm) deep and scraping soil from its side at a depth of 8–10 inches (20–25 cm). Then follow these steps:

Testing for Major Nutrients

1 Read completely and follow exactly all package label instructions for the reagent soil test kit.

2 Accurately measure the amount of soil required into the test tube, then add distilled water and drops of the kit's reagent. Shake the container.

3 Compare the color of the solution to the test kit's color panels, reading the result for each nutrient.

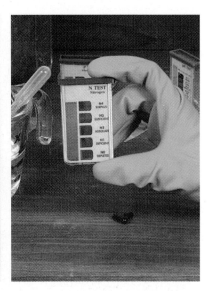

Testing for Acid-Alkaline Balance

1 Measure the soil's acid-alkaline balance with an electronic pH meter. Thoroughly mix your soil sample with distilled water, then allow it to settle.

2 Insert the meter's probe into the dissolved soil solution. Read the soil's pH on the instrument's needle or digital display.

3 The pH scale is neutral at 7.0, with lower numbers indicating acidic soil and higher numbers indicating alkaline soils. A pH of 6.0–7.0 suits most plants.

PLANNING FOR GARDEN CARE

Beyond beauty and wildlife, your garden plans should also take into account your own convenience. By allowing for this important aspect from the start, you'll have plenty of storage for equipment, supplies, and tools; plant-holding and potting areas; and spaces for working in and around your plants. Garden care will be easier, too.

Garden beds should have access paths through and behind them to make planting and seasonal care easier. Allow for work areas and provide access to tight spaces. Figure on a minimum width of 2 feet (60 cm) for paths around structures and among larger plant groupings. Although this may seem to be more space than necessary when gardens are young, the gaps will become less noticeable as your plants grow, mature, and fill in. Some plants, of course, need more care than others. If you choose to have a clipped hedge, for instance, allow room to access the length of the hedge to ease pruning, collection of pruned foliage, and removal. Remember, as you prune and weed, debris will accumulate and require collection; your access paths will make garden cleanup easier.

Also, allow for the care and cleaning of all your garden structures and your water feature. Provide easy access to electrical outlets, hose bibs, and faucets, or install new utility lines to service all areas of the wildlife garden. Include a nearby covered space for stretching out, hanging up, and storing garden hoses, buckets, and watering cans.

As you plan your pathways, consider using textural walking surfaces—a licorice root or cocoa hull mulch, perhaps, or a path of colored gravel—which look more natural than hard paving materials while providing visual interest, better traction, and increased personal safety for you and your visitors. Paths of tamped sand or fine rock over a weed-blocking barrier fabric and a base of gravel are good for low-traffic access, and they also permit water to drain through them into the gravel for runoff while preventing erosion. Think about installing structural walls and raised beds if you need to terrace hillsides to prevent soil from washing away or to create flat planting areas.

You'll also need areas for dry storage of supplies and tools as well as a potting area where you can keep extra containers and potting soil. Well-disguised trash and compost locations are necessities, too.

You may want to provide areas suitable for holding extra plants. It's sometimes difficult to obtain more of the same selected species or varieties later in the season, so it's a good idea to acquire a few extra shrubs and perennials, sink the containers into the soil, and add a layer of mulch. Or consider a cold frame, which is useful for holding frost-tender plants as well as for starting seed and overwintering hardy annuals, herbs, and perennials. For annual plants, herbs, and first-year perennials, set packs or pots into the cold frame, mulch around them, and keep them shaded when temperatures climb and direct sunlight is too intense for young foliage.

PROVIDING ACCESS PATHS

1 Make a photocopy of your garden plan, then fasten it to a work surface with drafting tape. Add a tracing paper overlay to begin your drawing.

Garden care is made easier when adequate walkways are part of your garden plan. Divide your garden's needs into those areas that need frequent or occasional access. Provide often-accessed areas with paths paved with non-skid, durable surfaces, such as fieldstone, masonry, or brick; finish seldom-used paths with crushed stone, bark, chips, or a durable ground cover, such as woolly thyme. Gather your base plan, tracing paper, drafting tape, and colored pencils, then follow these steps:

2 Establish a main access path through your garden by winding it around garden features. It should be 3–4 ft. (90–120 cm) wide.

3 Add lateral paths from the main walkway for access to seldom-used areas. They may be paved or unpaved, straight or curved, depending on your needs.

4 Make lateral paths in low-traffic areas 2½ ft. (75 cm) wide, frequently traveled paths 3 ft. (90 cm) wide.

5 Use colored pencils to indicate choices of paving and finishing materials for each path and add a legend for reference.

6 Calculate the area of each path by multiplying its length by its width. Note the measurements on your legend for reference when acquiring materials.

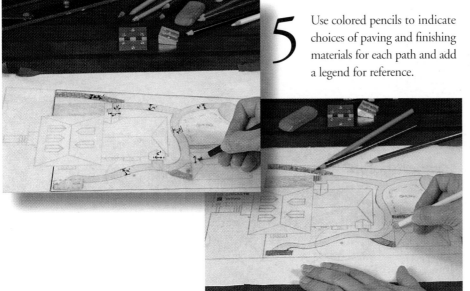

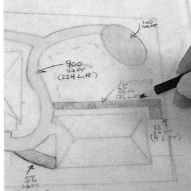

DESIGNING PLANTINGS

As you begin plant selection and placement, ask yourself these questions: "Do I want a sequence of blooms or fruit? Do I have specific colors, habits, or foliage preferences? Where will each plant be located?"

Because they anchor a garden, any large trees should be placed first. Whether evergreen or deciduous, trees are a good choice for wildlife. Many birds will perch, shelter, nest, and feed from trees such as beech, red cedar, fir, hemlock, oak, pine, spruce, sycamore, and black gum tupelo. Give trees the space they need to fully expand and spread by planting them the same distance apart as their mature height. Include smaller trees for more nesting, perching, and food sources. Mountain ash, birch, cherry, crabapple, dogwood, holly, cabbage palmetto, sumac, and willow are all good choices, depending on your climate.

Next, consider shrubs for your wildlife. Select at least five shrub species, choosing plants suited to low-light conditions for shade areas, then varieties for areas with ample light. Note their spacing, then count the number of plants needed. Landscapes look more natural when three to five plants of a species are irregularly grouped. Add irregular wavy lines of plants—called drifts—that intersect with access areas winding around or through the planted areas.

Many birds live on berries and fruits, so include barberry, cotoneaster, elderberry, holly, or berries such as raspberries and blueberries. Sketch your planting areas, indicate tree and shrub placement, and then make a list of needed plants.

Design the beds and borders of your bird or butterfly garden and choose plants for their habits, hardiness, bloom and fruiting seasons, and spacing requirements by consulting the encyclopedia in this and other references [see Encyclopedia of Popular Bird & Butterfly Plants, pg. 95].

BIRD & BUTTERFLY PLANTS

Plants for birds and butterflies include these easily grown choices:

Aster
Butterfly bush (*Buddleia*)
Chamomile
Columbine
Cosmos
Daylily
Feverfew
Grapes
Hawthorn
Honeysuckle
Juniper
Lilac
Milkweed (*Asclepias*)
Phlox
Purple coneflower
Rose
Salvia
Shasta daisy
Sunflower
Sweet alyssum
Wild cherry
Zinnia

CREATING FLOWER SUCCESSIONS

Chart the season of bloom for each plant you intend to include in your bird or butterfly garden. A simple plant succession chart will contain 12 vertical columns, one for each month. By double or triple planting areas of your garden, it's possible to have a continual succession of blooms. The bloom seasons for the plants will form the rows on the chart. Indicate bloom colors by using colored pencils. Gather graph paper, colored pencils, tracing paper, and plant information, then plan your flower successions by following these steps:

1 On graph paper, label 12 columns with the names of months, leaving space on the left for names of the plants. Choose your first plant, noting its bloom color and season.

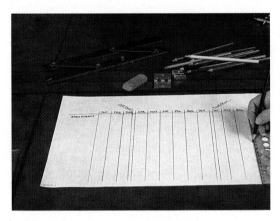

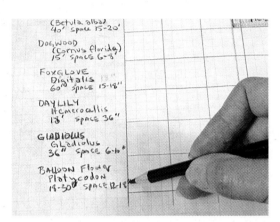

2 Note common and botanical names, plus any cultivar or variety name, for each plant. Also record all plant heights.

3 Select a colored pencil to match the bloom color. Fill in the span of columns matching the plant's bloom season in the row.

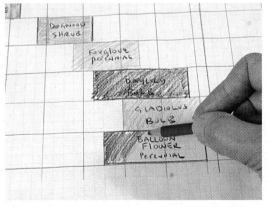

4 Continue until a row has been diagrammed for every plant. Create successions of early-, midseason-, and late-blooming plants with similar heights.

5 Prepare a tracing paper overlay to your garden plan. Match the plant successions with open spots in the garden's beds or borders.

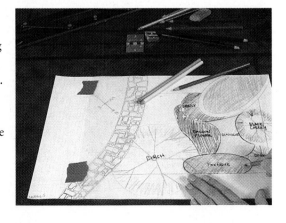

Garden Planting Basics

Now that you have planned your garden and you are imagining the enchanting sounds of birdsong, the flash and flutter of colorful wings, the shimmering colors of flowers, and the buzzing of a hummingbird right outside your window, you're probably eager to turn your dream garden into a living landscape. It's time to put your plan into action—gather the plants, materials, and supplies you need, and get started.

Moving from the planning stages to actually installing your bird or butterfly garden is exciting, fun, and a great way to enjoy your landscaping. Depending on your site, it can take a few hours, a day, a weekend, or several weekends to complete. If the site is large, consider installing your garden in stages, keeping the effort light and the results quick. For tasks that require strength, precision, or prior experience, think about seeking helpers from your family or friends, or hire professional landscapers.

You have already decided on the major improvements you'll make to your site, planning for planting beds, water features, low-voltage lighting systems, pathways, structures, and watering or irrigation systems. Now, you'll learn how they are installed. In the following pages you'll also find out how to prepare the soil by adding amendments. With step-by-step instructions, you'll see how to install a pond using a rigid, preformed liner and how to build a flower bed.

Next, you'll bring home ground covers, shrubs, trees and vines. You'll unload perennials, annuals in flats and packs, packets of seed, your soil amendments, and fertilizers. You'll first learn how to plant your landscape trees into the new garden areas, then the shrubs, and then add colorful perennial and annual flowers, both as nursery container plants and by sowing seed, with tips about their arrangement and early care. Finally, you'll water and mulch your new plantings.

As soon as you're finished and all of your plants are in the ground, you'll probably have a wildlife visitor nearby. And, as some time passes, more and more birds and butterflies will stop to enjoy the habitat you've created for them.

It's important to use the proper methods when you plant, whether for seed or for plants grown in nursery containers. You'll also need the right tools and supplies.

PREPARING TO PLANT

(Right) A mechanical tiller is useful for loosening the topsoil in your garden's beds. Remember that the tines of most tillers only penetrate 4–6 inches (10–15 cm) into the soil. It's always best to turn the soil at least 18 inches (45 cm) deep, usually with a shovel or spade.

(Below) The arrival of sustained warm weather means that it's time to plant trees, shrubs, and warm-season perennials. These plants grow best when warmth penetrates deep into the soil.

In creating any new or large planting areas, plan on doing all the necessary soil improvement and amendment first, once you've installed structures, systems, and permanent features. This is probably the only time you'll have full access to the area, and you'll want to make sure you're providing the new plants with the best possible start. However, keep in mind that trees generally should be planted directly in native rather than amended soil.

Get started by marking the planting areas using string and stakes. Dig in any needed soil amendments, plus humus, according to the recommendations of the soil tests you've done [see Analyzing Garden Soil, pg. 42]. You should allow the newly prepared soil to settle for a few days before you start to plant in the newly worked beds.

Now it's time to obtain your selected plants. Normally the season and weather are suitable for planting when you are able to obtain plants from your local garden nursery or retail garden center, or when direct retailers recommend receiving plants in your area. Wait to install them until all danger of late frosts has passed; for tender species, the ground should have warmed for several weeks.

It's a good idea to have on hand all the plants you'll need for the entire installation, or for one section if you have planned to install the garden in stages. Transport your plants to the garden site, protecting them from strong wind and hot sun during the trip. Water all the plants on arrival, and do so daily until they actually are in their final places.

On a wind-free day when temperatures in your garden are comfortable for digging and other planting tasks, set your plants in their approximate locations in each planting area and observe the design from every perspective and viewing angle. Try to imagine them at their full height. It may be helpful to use poles and ribbons or flags to help you picture the landscape after it matures. Move plants around as your sense of design may dictate, trying different arrangements until you are satisfied. Make your final adjustments now, when it's easiest to make changes.

AMENDING SOIL

1 Loosen the soil by spading the bed. For very compacted soil, double dig: excavate a trench 8–10 in. (25–30 cm) deep, then turn the soil at its base, so that the soil is loosened to 18 in. (45 cm) deep. Repeat across the entire bed.

Both fertilizers and soil amendments—additives that change the soil's texture or its acid-alkaline balance—are best added prior to planting. Conduct a soil test to decide the necessary quantities of fertilizer or amendment [see Soil Testing, pg. 43]. Organic fertilizers—well-rotted manure, compost, or natural minerals—slowly release their nutrients over time. Garden sulfur makes the soil more acidic, and lime increases its alkalinity; choose gypsum or organic compost for amending soil with too much clay or sand. Gather your fertilizer, amendments, shovel, rake, garden cart, respirator, and gloves, then follow these easy steps:

2 Spread rich, organic compost or well-rotted manure across the bed in a layer 3 in. (75 mm) deep. Spread with a rake until evenly dispersed.

3 Spread granular fertilizers with a rotary hand spreader. Carefully follow all fertilizer package instructions, and set the rate adjustment as directed by the manufacturer.

4 Apply gypsum, lime, or sulfur using a drop spreader. Carefully follow all package instructions, and set the rate adjustment as directed by the amendment manufacturer.

5 When all fertilizers and amendments are evenly spread, turn them into the soil with a spade, working at right angles to the original trenches or rows you dug.

6 Use a rake to level the soil surface, break up clods, remove any debris or rocks, and fill any depressions.

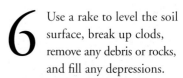

SITE CONSTRUCTION

Even if you expect that you will install your wildlife landscape in stages, put in the masonry, paving, utilities, and water features all at once to make the most of your materials and to conserve effort. Before actually constructing beds or garden features, obtain the necessary building permits or approvals from your local governmental agencies or neighborhood groups. Comply with all building code requirements, including installation of shutoff and antisiphon backflow-prevention valves for water lines and ground-fault circuit interrupters for outdoor

(Right) A border of marigolds is used frequently for softening the edge where a lawn meets a wall. Its flowers are midheight and bright in color, and can focus the eye on the neat division.

(Below) A small-space butterfly garden results when carefully selected plantings fill in a raised bed [see Building a Butterfly Flower Bed, next pg.].

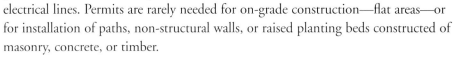

electrical lines. Permits are rarely needed for on-grade construction—flat areas—or for installation of paths, non-structural walls, or raised planting beds constructed of masonry, concrete, or timber.

Acquire all needed supplies such as cinder blocks, bricks, stone, sand, and timbers before you begin. If you'll use concrete, arrange for its delivery or plan to mix your own. For installing permanent features that require considerable effort or extra hands, line up helpers in advance or seek the help of a garden professional.

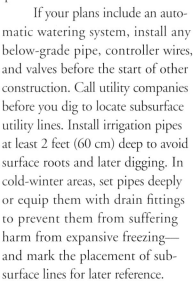

If your plans include an automatic watering system, install any below-grade pipe, controller wires, and valves before the start of other construction. Call utility companies before you dig to locate subsurface utility lines. Install irrigation pipes at least 2 feet (60 cm) deep to avoid surface roots and later digging. In cold-winter areas, set pipes deeply or equip them with drain fittings to prevent them from suffering harm from expansive freezing— and mark the placement of subsurface lines for later reference.

Protect existing large garden trees from mechanical damage, excavation of roots, or alteration of grade and drainage patterns; if you disrupt the root systems, disease and stress can result, even the loss of a tree. If amending your soil was postponed until after the features and systems were installed, now it's time to turn, amend, and fertilize the soil. Trees do best if planted directly in native soil; avoid amending soil when planting new trees.

BUILDING A
BUTTERFLY FLOWER BED

Butterfly gardens are colorful, pleasantly scented refuges grown within traditional landscape plantings. Setting aside an area for butterflies to gather, feed, and reproduce is easy. Here, field-stone boulders define a rough triangle and anchor a raised mound that will be planted. Gather flour, stakes, string, fieldstones, rich soil, a shovel, sand, gloves, then build your butterfly garden by following these steps:

1 Use the flour, stakes, and string to define an irregular triangle, about 50 sq. ft. (4.5 m²) in area, within an existing landscape bed or lawn.

2 In turfgrass areas, use a cutting tool to remove sod. Excavate holes about 8 in. (20 cm) deep at corners of the triangle and at a third the length of each side.

3 Fill each hole with a layer of bedding sand 3 in. (75 mm) deep. Place pairs of fieldstone boulders into each hole, rocking them into the sand.

4 Backfill the area with soil about 1 ft. (30 cm) deep. Allow the soil to spill around and through the boulders, sloping to the bed beyond the triangle.

5 Set a boulder in one corner of the butterfly bed. It will support a shallow water tray that may be filled later with moist sand for the butterflies.

INSTALLING A WATER FEATURE

Water is a powerful draw to birds and butterflies. You have many options for adding water to your landscape, from simple birdbaths to elaborate ponds and streams.

For smaller birds, a simple birdbath is ideal [see Self-Contained Birdbaths, this pg.]. The site should have good visibility, be safe from predators, and provide for easy access. Keep the water in the basin—up to an inch (25 mm) deep—fresh and clean. Very shallow water will attract butterflies—tailor the water level to their needs by adding some moist sand a bit higher than the planned water level.

Even tiny ponds will attract large bird populations and easily can create a focal point for your bird or butterfly garden. Small ponds are easiest to maintain, do a good job of holding their temperature and oxygen levels, and can be kept free of algae. Larger garden ponds may host aquatic plants, or their perimeters simply can be planted with moisture-loving plants. Flexible liners, available at home and garden retailers, are best for large ponds; use rigid preformed liners for smaller ponds. To include a fountain or waterfall, you'll also need a recirculating pump. If you install a pond with running water, plan for quiet areas free of splashing water. Natural stone and plants can add charm to these water features.

For large water features with fish, make your pond at least 3 feet (90 cm) deep. In cold-winter climates, it's best to extend the depth below ground-frost level, and avoid unlined concrete due to its likely cracking and water-quality changes. Instead, use flexible liners made of butyl or EPDM rubber—a tire-tube-like material. Include unusual aquatic plants, and add margin or bog plants to soften the edges of the pond. Stone edgings are also attractive. In cold winters, the pond may freeze nearly to its bottom—where the fish hibernate. Add floating blocks of foam plastic in autumn to protect the fish and prevent ice expansion from harming the liner.

Always consider safety when planning a water feature. Follow all local building codes and supervise children and pets to keep them safe from hazard.

SELF-CONTAINED BIRDBATHS

Building a birdbath is a great family project that provides enjoyable returns for many years. You can find everything you need at most home and garden retailers. For permanent installations, place the feature on a concrete footing. Then choose a bowl or basin, and a recirculating pump or bubbler. Recycling the water makes caring for the birdbath easier and extends the time between cleanings, while the sound of water dripping or flowing will appeal to birds. If you are located in a cold-winter climate, add a heating element to keep the water in the birdbath from freezing or drain it. You will need to either permanently wire the bath or plug its water pump into a weatherproof, GFCI-protected outlet.

(Above) If you have limited space, take advantage of eaves on your home or limbs of a tree to hang a suspended birdbath.

(Below) Depending on your yard, you may have room for a larger water feature such as this pond surrounded by boulder coping stones and traversed by a wooden bridge joining two paths.

INSTALLING A GARDEN POND

Installing a garden pond using a rigid, preformed liner requires excavating a hole whose dimensions, depths, and slopes match exactly those of the liner. After digging, add an underlay of sand to help support the liner, then follow these steps:

1 Gently set the liner in place, making sure its bottom and shelves are set evenly and the liner's lip is flush with the level excavated area.

2 Check the level across the pond's length and breadth. To adjust, press down firmly in high points, or add and remove sand as required for a good fit.

3 Fill around the liner's sides and rim. Avoid disturbing the liner's position and level. If the water feature is large, use a long straight-edge to span the feature's sides.

4 Compact the margins alongside the liner, using a tamping tool. Maintain an even level along the perimeter.

5 Add water to the liner. Use a sump pump to remove any sediment. Install a submersible recirculating pump. If desired, add a fountainhead.

6 Trial fit your coping stones or other edging materials to cover the liner. They will protect the edges from sun damage.

PLANTING TREES AND SHRUBS

When you obtain trees and shrubs, they may be bare root, balled-and-burlapped—often called "B-and-B"—or container grown. Bare-root plants are dormant and should be planted immediately; B-and-B plants will hold for several weeks; and container plants will keep for months—but the sooner all are in the ground, the sooner they'll become established and grow. Plant your large trees first, then smaller trees, and finally shrubs.

The planting method is essentially the same for any size tree or shrub. Shrubs should be set in amended soil, while trees are best planted in native soil. It's easiest to determine the size of the planting hole for balled-and-burlapped or container-grown stock. Make their holes 6–12 inches (15–30 cm) wider than the outside diameter and as deep as the rootball. Plant bare-root plants in holes 2 feet (60 cm) wide and deep.

Always loosen the soil in the planting hole below the soil that you remove, because it's likely to be hardpan—an impervious layer of heavy clay. For shrubs only, mix your amendments with the native soil. Trim any broken roots from the plant, and set it into the hole to the same depth as it was grown, noting the discolored soil line on its trunk. With a helper holding the tree or shrub upright, fill in around the roots or rootball with soil removed from the hole, a shovel of soil at a time. Tamp the soil firm around the roots. When the hole is nearly full, add a gallon (3.8 l) of fresh water. Allow it to be absorbed, then repeat with additional water.

Avoid staking small trees and shrubs. For larger trees, install stakes until their roots become established and their trunks gain strength—usually two seasons. Use heavy-gauge wire wrapped with an old piece of bike tire, and two 2×2 (38×38-mm) wooden posts, 6 feet (1.8 m) long, spaced on opposite sides of the tree and set 2 feet (60 cm) into the soil. Loosely attach the ties near the tree's crown branches, allowing some movement. Apply at least a gallon (3.8 l) of water per plant per day until new growth begins.

After allowing the soil to settle for several weeks, top off the hole until it is level with the surrounding ground. Spread a layer of organic mulch 3 inches (75 mm) thick, keeping the mulch at least 3 inches (75 mm) from the trunks. Fertilize with a balanced mix of liquid fertilizer—one that is formulated with equal amounts of nitrogen, phosphorus, and potassium and is labeled 10–10–10, for instance—or use a slow-release fertilizer spread around the plant's drip line, the soil directly beneath its outermost branches. Always read completely and follow exactly all fertilizer label instructions.

Essential tools for planting trees and shrubs include a wheelbarrow filled with mulch, a shovel, and a garden rake. Keep in mind that trees in large nursery containers and boxes are heavy. Arrange help to transport them to your planting site.

PLANTING NURSERY CONTAINER PLANTS

1 Dig a planting hole and gently remove the plant from its nursery container. Before you plant, check its roots; if rootbound, loosen them with your fingers or a hand fork.

When planting in unimproved soil around existing trees or shrubs, dig the planting hole 2–3 times as wide as the nursery container and 18 inches (45 cm) deep. Add amendments to the removed soil and backfill to the proper planting depth so the new plant will be surrounded with improved soil. In a previously amended bed, the hole should be as deep as the nursery container and 1½ times its width. Use care to avoid disturbing existing roots. To plant perennials from nursery containers into a bed or border, follow these steps:

2 Set the plant in the hole. If the soil is undisturbed, place the top of the rootball even with surrounding soil. In loose, amended soil, set it 1 in. (25 mm) above nearby soil.

3 Fill the hole halfway with soil. Firm the soil lightly using your palms. Fill all remaining space around the plant with soil, to the top of its rootball.

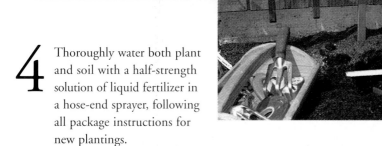

4 Thoroughly water both plant and soil with a half-strength solution of liquid fertilizer in a hose-end sprayer, following all package instructions for new plantings.

5 Allow the soil to settle. Add organic mulch around each plant in a layer 3 in. (75 mm) deep. Keep mulch at least 3 in. (75 mm) from the plant's stem at the base.

6 Support when needed with a trellis or plant stake. Loosely tie the plant's stem or vining branches to a stake or lattice, allowing for about 1–2 in. (25–50 mm) of movement.

PLANTING BEDDING PLANTS AND SEED

When planting nursery-grown perennial plants and annuals or raising flowering plants from seed, put them in after all trees, shrubs, and bulbs have been planted. They are available as container-grown, bare-root, or pack-grown plants or plugs. Container-grown plants can be held for several weeks; bare-root plants, plugs, and packs should be planted immediately.

Plant the tallest plants first, at the center of an island bed or at the back of a border, and then fill the remaining space by planting progressively shorter varieties as you move to the edges or front. Space the plants as recommended for each species. For drifts, it's easiest to plant in a trench; to set individual plants, dig separate holes for each. Make each hole 2–4 inches (50–100 mm) larger all the way around than the root-ball of the plant. Set the plant in the hole at the same level it was in the pot or in the ground, and then fill with removed soil. Firm the soil around each plant with your palm, and apply several quarts (liters) of water to each plant. Let it soak in, then water again. When you've finished planting, add a layer of organic mulch over the soil around the plants to help keep the soil evenly moist and reduce weeds. Maintain an open area, 1–2 inches (25–50 mm) wide, away from the plant stems. Water daily until new growth begins.

An economical way to obtain abundant color and stretch your budget is to plant seed. Annuals are particularly rewarding and simple to grow. Plant sun-loving annuals in full sun; choose partial-shade areas for plants requiring some sun protection. Read completely and follow all seed package directions. For best results, always plant at the package-recommended depth.

Sow seed such as bachelor button, cosmos, larkspur, marigold, sweet William, and zinnia directly in garden soil, planting them last. Scatter seed, press it into soil, and cover it with a fine sifting of soil if so directed. Keep the seedbed evenly moist with a hand mister until plants emerge and have several sets of true leaves. Then thin the seedlings to the recommended spacing for the species or gently dig, move, and relocate them.

Seed is a quick and easy way to add color to your garden. Prepare the soil by adding fertilizer and amendments, then raking it until it is smooth. Remove any mulch, debris, or clods. Always consult the seed packet for depth and plant spacing recommendations.

PLANTING FLOWERS

Spacing is important for bedding plants and flowers grown from seed. Consult the plant encyclopedia for spacing information [see Encyclopedia of Bird and Butterfly Plants, pg. 95]. Bedding plants are offered in packs as well as in 4- or 6-inch (10- or 15-cm) pots. Gather plants or seed, ruler, trowel, hand rake, organic compost, watering can, and gloves, then follow these steps:

Planting Bedding Plants

1 In a fertilized and amended bed, space plants as recommended. Dig a hole as deep and wide as each plant's growing container.

2 Flex the container, then gently remove the plant by pushing up on the rootball, avoiding pulling on the stem.

3 Set each plant into a hole, then compact the soil around it with your open palms to ensure good contact. Water the plants.

Planting Seed

1 In a fertilized and amended bed, rake the surface smooth. Scatter seed onto the soil at the recommended spacing.

2 Note the desired planting depth from the seed package. Cover the seeds lightly with organic compost to the recommended depth, then firm the soil over them. Mark the planting.

3 Using a watering can fitted with a diffusing rose, gently moisten the planting. Keep the bed evenly moist until seeds germinate and sprouts emerge.

Butterflies

The joy of butterflies in the garden has inspired poets for ages. These winged jewels are so varied in their size and color, so thrilling to watch, that even the most beautiful ground-bound plants provide only a backdrop to their motion. Some butterflies have picturesque common names such as hairstreak and snout. Their scientific names are equally fascinating: the eyed brown satyr's, for instance, is *Lethe eurydice*, conjured straight out of Greek mythology.

Get in on all this excitement by familiarizing yourself with those things that butterflies need, and then plant some surefire attractants around your home. More than 10,000 species in the order LEPIDOPTERA are found in North America alone. Butterflies, skippers, and moths have unique scaled wings that give them the brilliance, even iridescence, found only in these species. You can learn to identify them by their differences. Most butterflies have slim, hairless bodies and antennae with clublike balls on or near the tips.

Skippers, usually dark in color, have thicker, hairier bodies with hooks at the end of their antennae. Both are active during the day. Moths have varying antenna shapes without clublike ends, and most appear feathery.

There are some spectacular moth species. However, most moths are nocturnal and many are serious plant pests. Only a few butterflies and their relatives—cabbage, mourning cloak, and alfalfa among them—are considered plant pests. Some species migrate thousands of miles to lay their eggs and die, while their offspring magically retain the instinctive ability to return to the place where their parents fed and mated.

In this chapter, you'll be introduced to some of the most common North American butterflies. You can expand your knowledge about specific species in your region by consulting field guides or electronic information sources. You'll also learn about plants that serve as food sources for adults—nectar producers—and other favorite food sources for caterpillars—butterfly host plants.

The more you learn about butterflies, the more enjoyment you'll receive from them. Get the family excited about this living overlay of color and motion, and then start watching regularly for visitors to your garden.

Discover the basics of butterfly life to learn how best to draw these beautiful creatures to your garden where you can observe them

The giant swallowtail is one of the largest North American butterfly species, with a wingspan that often reaches 5 inches (13 cm). Its preferred host plants are prickly ash, citrus, and rue, although swallowtails sometimes are drawn to conifers, as shown here.

ATTRACTING BUTTERFLIES

It's easy, fascinating, and educational to attract certain butterfly species to your garden areas by offering everything they require to complete their life cycle. You most likely will have the greatest success when you try to attract butterflies that are common native species in your region, rather than rare, unusual, or distant species. As a conscientious gardener, always keep in mind that exotic species may compete with native butterflies, and your plants, lacking resistance, may be damaged by them. If you concentrate on butterflies common in your area, you'll maintain the natural environment and still have encounters with many species.

Consider the requirements of a butterfly garden. To provide a complete butterfly habitat, include these simple elements: a shallow source of water, wind protection and shelter, areas away from foot or pet traffic, and a sunny zone with an assortment of trees, shrubs, and flowering plants for fragrance, color, nectar, and food [see Butterflies and Host Plants, pg. 68–69]. Also, when you garden for butterflies—indeed, for any wildlife—it's important to use only organic and environmentally friendly gardening techniques, which are essential to maintain the health of all the life stages of the butterflies present in your landscape [see Gardening with Nature, pg. 71].

An attractively planned habitat will bring butterflies to your landscape, and the necessary host plants will encourage the adults to stay, mate, and lay eggs in your garden. These are the aims of the butterfly gardener: ensuring reproduction, maturity, and another generation—probably many—of the same species. Migrating species emerging in your garden may also return.

Common North American butterflies you may see, depending on your location, are admirals, anglewings, blues, buckeyes, checkerspots, coppers, crescents, elfins, emperors, fritillaries, hairstreaks, painted ladies, metalmarks, monarchs, mourning cloaks, satyrs, skippers, sulphurs, swallowtails, and whites. Showy moths include the cecropia, imperial, io, luna, polyphemus, sphinx, and royal walnut.

(Below left) A red-spotted purple, the southern subspecies of the closely similar white admiral. As for all butterflies, the striking color patterns we see are caused by optical refraction patterns on its tiny scales.

(Below right) Likely to be the most recognized and popular insect in North America, the monarch migrates long distances and gathers in huge numbers during winter along the Pacific coast, Baja California, and in the highlands of Mexico.

OBSERVING NATIVE SPECIES

Butterflies are identified most easily by their wing color, pattern, and size. Field guides contain this key information. Visit nature centers and join nature clubs in your area; some offer field trips that will help you understand butterfly activity. You'll also begin looking at the plants they visit as clues to identifying them. Record your sightings, with notes on plant, butterfly, stage, dates, and first and last sightings of the season. Take photos to record butterflies you see along with the plants on which they are feeding, laying their eggs, or resting.

CHOOSING FLOWERS FOR BUTTERFLIES

Nectar-producing flowers attract butterflies with color, scent, and promise of food. Butterflies generally prefer flat, open-faced flowers that provide a good spot for resting and feeding, or deep-throated flowers that hold abundant nectar. Consult the plant encyclopedia [see Encyclopedia of Popular Bird and Butterfly Plants, pg. 95] as you choose the flowers for your butterfly garden. Pick plants by selecting those with butterfly-attracting features:

A Flowering shrubs with clusters of nectar-bearing flowers borne midspring–summer such as crape myrtle (shown here), wild cherry, or honey locust.

B Perennial flowering shrubs with strong, sweet scents and bright flowers such as butterfly bush (shown here) and lilac.

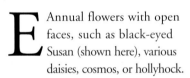

C Flowering vines with large, deep-throated flowers such as honeysuckle, mandevilla, morning glory (shown here), and wisteria.

D Perennial flowers with daisy-like faces, including Shasta daisy and purple coneflower (shown here).

E Annual flowers with open faces, such as black-eyed Susan (shown here), various daisies, cosmos, or hollyhock.

F Deep-throated flowers filled with nectar, including butterfly weed, monkey flower, nasturtium, and snapdragon.

HOST PLANTS

Butterflies lay eggs on host plants that their hatching larvae will use as food sources. The female deposits her eggs where the offspring can begin eating immediately after they hatch. Butterfly eggs are adhesive, and they may be laid singly, in clusters, in rows, or in masses, usually on the undersides of the leaves.

The caterpillar stage of various species of butterflies is identifiable and fun to observe. It's important to be able to identify the caterpillar of your butterfly species to avoid possible confusion with unwanted garden pests; a good field guide is a useful reference. Caterpillars do eat their host plants. Over time, these plants may become a little raggedy, perhaps even entirely devoured. Anticipate this by planting your host plants in large masses, reserving some in other areas of your garden for transplant when necessary, or holding extra host plants in a cold frame. Place these plants in inconspicuous locations in your butterfly landscape where other foliage will hide their chewed state. Or you can carefully prune the plants—after the caterpillars have passed into their pupa stage—being careful to avoid cutting off any branches that bear a chrysalis. Many trees also provide hosting for butterfly larvae, but the impact on leaves in tall branches may be less apparent than that which can be seen easily on nearby, smaller flowering plants where chewed leaves are apparent.

Butterfly–host plant relationships can be very specific. Many butterflies have a specially adapted anatomy, which causes them to be dependent on only one or two host plants [see Butterflies and Host Plants, pg. 68–69]. These plants are crucial to the survival of their species through all four stages of their life cycle. For example, for swallowtails, include carrots, fennel, and parsley; for the monarchs, milkweed-family plants (there are quite a few varieties from which to choose); for painted lady, hollyhock and mallow. By providing the right host plants in your butterfly garden for egg-laying and as a supply of food for their caterpillars, you'll help to ensure a continuing butterfly population in your landscape. When there's a specific butterfly species that you enjoy, you can choose from among its known host plants to ensure the sustenance and rearing of its young, and you'll be making a contribution to keeping the population healthy and will be providing new generations of butterflies for people to enjoy—today and in the years to come.

(Right) Hibiscus, a woody, flowering tropical plant that is tender in times of frost, often is grown as a container plant. Its fiery red blossoms are a sure lure for many species of butterfly, as well as hummingbirds.

(Far right) Milkweed—also called butterfly weed—is an attractive host plant to monarch butterflies.

GROWING A BUTTERFLY NURSERY

Native host plants attract local butterflies by offering them places to lay their eggs and rear their young. Host plants include certain landscape shrubs and flowers, grasses, trees, and wild plants such as milkweed, thistle, and nettle [see Butterflies and Host Plants, pgs. 68–69]. Your garden will attract butterflies from far away if you plant these and other hosts. Gather your plants, trellises, lattice, shovel, hand trowel, and gloves, then follow these steps:

1 Install trellises in your beds to help support climbing vines. Add lattice windbreaks if your site is subject to strong winds.

2 Observe how shadows fall on the bed. Plant host shrubs and trees in spots that avoid shading other plantings.

3 Plant the tallest host plant species in the center of beds or in the background of borders.

4 Between the vines, tall plants, shrubs, and trees, mix short and midsized plantings. Plant smallest species at the bed or border margins.

5 Note whenever butterflies visit your nursery. Look closely for egg masses on the undersides of leaves after they depart.

SHELTER
AND REFUGE

Adult butterflies are intent on feeding from nectar flowers, mating, and egg-laying. Imagine what a strong gust of wind or a sudden downpour might do to interfere with their intentions. Because they are fragile and lightweight, adults need refuge areas where they can rest, away from strong winds and protected from rain. During wet weather, butterflies rest in trees and shrubs, under large leaves, on the undersides of large branches, under home eaves, and in tree hollows. Then they re-emerge when the sun comes out, winds pass, and temperatures warm.

As you plan for shelter and refuge, consider the chance to accommodate areas of respite, as well as those of provision. Large trees and thickly branching shrubs will offer sheltered resting places. Adult butterflies enjoy basking in the sun. A board, flat stone, or sandy area in a full-sun location is good for that purpose. Be sure that you also include areas with food plants that are sheltered from wind [see Wind Protection, this pg.].

WIND PROTECTION

Butterflies may have difficulty when flying, landing, feeding, or sheltering in windy regions. Plant an area with blooming plants protected from prevailing winds and gusting breezes to encourage them to enter your garden. Use fieldstones to create a dry-stack garden wall. Plant on a gentle leeward slope. Install a hedge trimmed 3–4 ft. (90–120 cm) tall, or build a fence of the same height; either will protect from wind a horizontal area as great as ten times its height. Group evergreen trees and shrubs upwind from your butterfly plants. Periodically observe your butterfly sites on windy days. Structures and natural plant growth may alter wind direction or strength as time passes.

Some butterfly species live through the winter in mild-winter climate regions. Remember as you do your autumn garden cleanup that butterflies may be sheltering on the plants or leaves within your landscape, especially those that also are host plants. Keep an eye out for any egg deposits or pupa cases that might have been laid by adult butterflies to overwinter in your garden. Avoid pruning limbs to which they have been attached. Provide additional hibernation areas—a coffee can that has been half-filled with dry leaves and then placed securely and horizontally in the crotch of a tree can become an enticing shelter for many adult butterflies, including mourning cloak, painted lady, and red admiral.

(Above) Gathered monarchs flock to gum eucalyptus trees; they are seen throughout southern California and Mexico during the winter months.

(Right) Consider building your butterfly garden in concentric rings, using the outer perimeter plantings for walls, tall trees, and high hedges. The center of the circle will be protected from winds of all directions.

A SHELTER FOR BUTTERFLY METAMORPHOSIS

A fter hatching from eggs, butterflies continue their lives as larvae, or caterpillars. Young larvae are voracious eaters—they double in size every day or two. Many species shed their skin several times as they grow. In a final act, the caterpillar attaches itself to a woody stem, leaf, or other object and turns into a chrysalis, from which the mature butterfly will emerge. To have abundant butterflies in your garden, look for and protect butterflies in their chrysalis form at locations such as the following:

A Attached to the undersides of tree limbs and twigs near their joint with the trunk or a larger branch.

B Hanging beneath leaves of host plants in a dry, sheltered location, or in the foliage of trees and shrubs. Look for chewed leaves or silky webbing.

C On foliage, stems, and leaves of plants found growing near the butterfly's host plants. Often camouflaged.

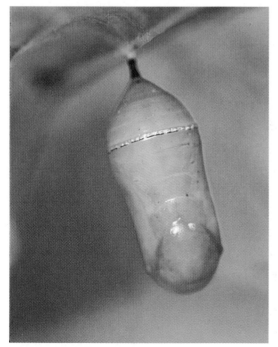

D On the undersides of logs or wood in woodpiles found near butterfly host plants.

BUTTERFLIES AND HOST PLANTS

This list contains a number of common North American butterfly and colorful moth species that you may see in your local area, along with the preferred plants where they lay their eggs.

Common Name	Scientific Name	Common Host Plants
BUTTERFLIES		
American Copper	*Lycaena hypophlaeas*	Sheep sorrel
American Painted Lady	*Vanessa virginiensis*	Buckeye, hollyhock, *Junonia coenia*, mimulus, snapdragon, plantain, thistle, verbena
American Snout	*Libytheana carinenta*	Hackberry, violet
Anicia Checkerspot	*Euphydryas chalcedona*	Figwort (SCROPHULARIACEAE), snowberry
Anise Swallowtail	*Papilio zelicaon*	Carrot, lemon, lime, orange
Appalachian Eyed Brown	*Satyrodes appalachia*	Sedges
Atlantis Fritillary	*Speyeria atlantis*	Violet
Baltimore	*Euphydryas phaeton*	Plantain, turtlehead (*Chelone glabra*)
Banded Hairstreak	*Satyrium calanus*	Oak, nuts
Black Swallowtail (Easter Tiger Swallowtail)	*Papilio polyxenes*	Carrot
Brown Elfin	*Incisalia augustinus*	Blueberry, lilac
Buckeye	*Junonia coenia*	Snapdragon, vervain
Cabbage White	*Pieris rapae*	Cabbage, mustard, nasturtium
California Sister	*Limenitis bredowii*	Oak
Checkered White	*Pontia protodice*	Mustard
Clouded Sulfur	*Colias philodice*	Clover, legumes, marigold
Cloudless Sulfur	*Phoebis sennae*	Senna (*Cassia* species)
Comma	*Polygonia comma*	Hops, nettle
Common Snout (American Snout)	*Libytheana carinenta* (*Libytheana bachmanii*)	Hackberry, violet
Common Wood Nymph	*Cercyonis pegala*	Grasses
Coral Hairstreak	*Satyrium titus*	Cherry, plum
Eastern Tailed Blue	*Everes comyntas*	Legume
Eastern Tiger Swallowtail (Black Swallowtail)	*Papilio polyxenes*	Carrot
Eyed Brown Satyr	*Lethe eurydice*	Grasses
Giant Swallowtail	*Paplio cresphontes* (*Heraclides cresphontes*)	Prickly ash, citrus, rue
Gray Hairstreak	*Strymon melinus*	Cactus, corn, hops, legumes, mallow, mint, snapdragon, strawberry
Gulf Fritillary	*Agraulis vanillae*	Passionflower, violet, willow

Common Name	Scientific Name	Common Host Plants
Harvester	*Feniseca tarquinius*	Only carnivorous butterfly (feeds on aphids, plantlice)
Little Copper	*Lycaena phlaeas*	Sheep sorrel
Little Yellow	*Eurema lisa*	Legumes
Meadow Fritillary	*Boloria bellona*	Violet
Monarch	*Danaus plexippus*	Milkweed
Mourning Cloak	*Nymphalis antiopa*	Birch, cottonwood, elm, hackberry, poplar, willow
Mylitta Crescent	*Phyciodes mylitta*	Aster, thistle
Olive Hairstreak	*Mitoura grynea*	Cedar
Orange Sulfur	*Colias eurytheme*	Alfalfa, clover, legumes, marigold
Painted Lady	*Vanessa cardui*	Daisy, thistle
Pearl Crescent	*Phyciodes tharos*	Aster
Queen	*Danaus gilippus*	Milkweed
Question Mark	*Polygonia interrogationis*	Elm, hackberry, hops
Red Admiral	*Vanessa atalanta*	Nettle, false nettle
Red-Spotted Purple	*Limenitis arthemis* subsp. *astyanax*	Cherry, poplar, willow
Satyr	*Polygonia satyrus*	Nettle
Silvery Blue	*Glaucopsyche lygdamus*	Legumes
Southern Dogface	*Colias cesonia*	Clover, legumes
Spicebush Swallowtail	*Papilio troilus*	Sassafras, spicebush *(Lindera benzoin)*
Spring Azure	*Celestrina ladon (C. argiolus)*	Blueberry, *Ceanothus* species, dogwood, lupine, viburnum
Variegated Fritillary	*Euptoieta claudia*	Passionflower, violet
Veined White	*Pieris napi*	Mustard
Viceroy	*Limenitis archippus*	Cherry, milkweed, poplar, willow
Western Tiger Swallowtail	*Papilio rutulus*	Hops, poplar, willow
Zebra Swallowtail	*Eurytides marcellus*	Pawpaw

NOTABLE MOTHS

Cecropia	*Hyalophora cecropia*	Apple, cherry, elderberry, maple, plum
Five-Spotted Hawk Sphinx	*Protoparche quinquemaculata*	Phlox, tomato
Io	*Automaris io*	Corn, rose
Luna	*Actias luna*	White birch, sweet gum, persimmon, black walnut, willow

BUTTERFLY LIFE HISTORY

Learn to recognize each of the life forms of butterflies. You'll likely find them in all stages of development. Members of LEPIDOPTERA, the order of butterflies and moths, have a four-stage life cycle, yet the creature in each developmental form bears little similarity to the others.

After mating, adult females lay eggs on host plants. Eggs are quite different from species to species, are adhesive, and sometimes are laid in patterns on leaves, stems, or even on the ground. Some eggs hatch in a few days; others are deposited in autumn to hatch in spring. Hatchlings technically are called larvae, or more commonly, caterpillars. They are distinctive; some—such as swallowtail caterpillars and tomato hornworms—are remarkable in coloration or size.

A caterpillar's sole aim is to eat its way to maturity. Over a period lasting from a week to several months, it repeatedly sheds its skin, emerging each time as a larger caterpillar. The caterpillar then begins to pupate, wrapping itself in a unique case—called a chrysalis—that is well-camouflaged. Some pupae hang from stems, some roll into leaves, and some—cocoon-like—are found on the ground amid fallen leaves. The pupa of each species is unique. With experience, you may be able to recognize the chrysalides of many common types of butterflies, and you'll find yourself wondering at the changes that are taking place inside each insect's case.

During this remarkable transformation, the body cells within the larva begin to migrate, reassembling themselves in other places to form the adult's wings, head, antennae, thorax, and legs. This may take a few days, a dry summer, or an entire winter. When the butterfly has matured, it slowly breaks open its pupal case and emerges. Within an hour, the adult's wings will have filled with fluid, dried, and hardened. With the flap of its wings, it takes to the air for the first time, free forever of its previous earthbound existence.

Adults may live several months, a season, or longer. Some migrate in large groups to distant areas to feed and mate, while others overwinter on plants in your landscape. Still others produce several generations each season.

Three of the four steps in the life of a monarch butterfly follow the hatching of its eggs: the larva, or caterpillar (top); chrysalis and metamorphosis (middle top); and the emerging adult, its wings still damp and folded (middle bottom). This adult is ready for flight (bottom).

CATERPILLARS

Once you know their appearance, caterpillars are easy to identify and fun to look for under leaves, on stems, and on flowers. Identify each species by the plant upon which it feeds. The monarch, for example, usually is found on plants of the milkweed family. You might observe, identify, or collect caterpillars of native species. To collect caterpillars and keep them healthy, snip off the plant parts where you find them and place them in a breathable, covered box for prompt transport to your garden, where you'll place them on host plants of the same species. Remember, insect collection is prohibited in most parks and nature preserves. In other areas, collect only common native species; avoid all that are rare or endangered.

When you plant for birds and butterflies, many insects already will be in your garden. Most are harmless or even beneficial, but to limit hazard to your nectar-producing and host plants, you may need to manage a few pests. Use only organic and manual control methods to ensure the safety of visiting birds and butterflies.

GARDENING WITH NATURE

Keep your plants pest- and disease-free by providing regular care. Plant each species in small groups in several different beds; divided plantings help limit pest populations. Water and fertilize regularly to keep your plants in peak condition. Perform quick, weekly garden inspections; that way, you'll be sure to notice any new insects and diseases. Plant diseases often appear right after an insect infestation. If you find pests, step in right away before plants become defoliated or stunted.

Control is easier if you know pest habits—slugs and snails, for instance, emerge at night and remain until early morning. Hand pick them and crush them underfoot, or place them in a killing jar containing dilute denatured ethyl alcohol or soapy water mixed with household ammonia. For insects, wash infested plants with a strong stream of plain water. You also can introduce beneficial insects such as ladybird beetles, lacewings, and praying mantises that will feed on many pest and nuisance insects.

For infestations that continue after hand picking and washing, either accept minor loss of plant foliage; use a solution of insecticidal soap to spot-treat identified pest eggs, grubs, or adults; or apply *Bacillus thuringiensis* (BT) directly to the target pest as a spot application using a cotton swab. Avoid widespread application of soaps or BT, however, as it also will harm butterfly larvae and beneficial insects in your garden. Wear protective clothing and gloves, and always read completely and follow exactly all of the package-label directions.

As with pests, forethought is the best defense against disease. Avoid practices that encourage fungal disease—overhead watering that splashes plant foliage and watering late in the day, for instance. Note when diseases first appear, and pick your fight; you might ignore mildew on lilacs for instance—it's pretty much a fact of life—while removing a plant with incurable mosaic virus. Prune off any of the diseased plant parts, removing them from your garden, and always be sure to disinfect your pruning shears by dipping them into dilute rubbing alcohol solution after each cut.

Three natural control methods: releasing ladybird beetles— ladybugs—voracious predators that eat many smaller insects (above); dusting aphids from flowers and foliage with a fine brush (left); solarizing soil to kill harmful nematodes (bottom).

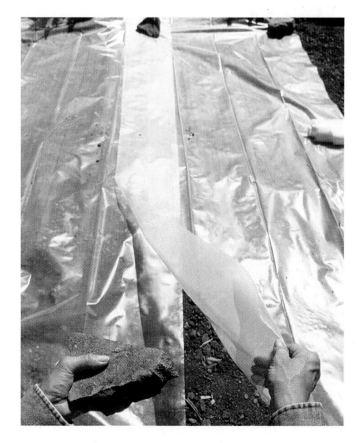

Birds will amaze and fascinate you with their variety, habits, and beauty. When you invite birds into your garden, you'll experience an ongoing song and dance, changing from season to season, from year to year, but everlasting. In spring, you'll see migratory birds returning, mating, and raising families. You'll watch the hatchlings as they grow and flit through your garden areas, eating bugs and singing their concerts for you to enjoy. In summer, you may see hummingbirds, and possibly second broods of songbirds. In autumn, you'll watch for the change of focus as migratory birds begin to leave or arrive from other regions.

Watching the seasons change along with the birds in your garden brings a wonderful sense of continuity. Your whole family will be interested in watching and feeding birds in and around the yard. You'll be involved in a healthful and fascinating pastime—one of the most popular nature hobbies. There is vast variety in the world of birds—from hummingbirds to vultures—and there are many opportunities to learn and observe more about the particular birds native to your local area.

You have already explored ways you can introduce plants and features into your landscape that birds will find irresistible. In the following pages, you'll learn about the many different birds you may invite and watch in your landscape, depending on your location.

In this chapter you'll discover information about the feeding and nesting preferences of many common species of North American hummingbirds, songbirds, and other colorful species so you can attract them to your garden. You'll also learn about special winter feeding needs. Step by step, you'll see how to plant deep-throated flowers, install hanging feeders and make artifical nectar for your hummingbirds, adapt a gourd as a birdhouse, make specialized feeding stations, and build a backyard blind. Finally, you'll learn how to identify, observe, and even photograph your bird visitors as they come and go.

Study the basics of bird behavior to learn how best to lure winged visitors to your backyard for a close-up look

Backyard Birds

A female eastern bluebird, pausing atop a rain gauge after catching its prey, reveals much about its behaviorial traits. The time it spent closely examining its watcher allowed time for this remarkable portrait. In this chapter, you'll receive many tips on watching birds and bird photography.

ATTRACTING HUMMINGBIRDS

These tiny, iridescent, whirring wonders are such a reward in your landscape. Plan to include a few of their favorite plants and roll out a red carpet of flowers—literally, because red attracts hummingbirds. If you add a water source, trees, vines, and flowering plants at least 2 feet (60 cm) high, hummingbirds will certainly come to your garden.

All hummingbird species are migratory to some degree, with a few flying as far as

600 miles (966 km) as they follow the successive bloom of their food plants. Flowers with long, tubular forms seem made for hummingbirds, with specially designed bills for drinking flower nectar. With unusually strong wing muscles—hummingbirds beat their wings between 20 and 200 times per second and flex them at different angles—they hover before a flower. They dart their specialized, long, and needlelike bills into the flower's nectaries, extend their long tongues, and quickly drink. Their extremely high metabolism rate requires them to constantly replenish their bodies with high-energy food and water throughout the day. Their favorite plants include cardinal flower, fuchsia, honeysuckle, morning glory, penstemon, salvia, and trumpet vine.

Nectar from flowering plants is a natural choice, but hummingbirds also are attracted to feeders filled with nectar solution [see Artificial Nectar, next pg.]. Because hummingbirds are fiercely territorial, spread several feeders around the garden out of sight of one another. For easy viewing near a window, plant a window box, hang a feeder, or dangle a basket of brightly colored flowers—hummingbirds are drawn to pink and orange in addition to red.

Hummingbirds augment their diets with insects and spiders and will drink sap as it runs from trees. They also need water—as much as eight times their body weight each day—so place feeders near water.

Trees and shrubs are good nesting spots for these tiny birds. With moss, fiber from plants, feathers, and spider webs, females build nests—1 inch (25 mm) across and deep—amid their protective branches.

(Top) Red, deep-throated flowers such as fuchsia are an irresistible draw to all hummingbirds. With a whir, an Anna's hummingbird takes a sip from the flower.

(Right) This Costa's hummingbird will take a matter of moments to sample the nectar from each of the individual flowers in this cluster.

INSTALLING HANGING FEEDERS AND PLANTS

Several options exist when installing hanging planters and feeders—you can hang them from trees, existing structures, or pole supports. Some of the methods shown here are suitable for discouraging squirrels or other foraging wildlife from raiding feeders. Choose the option that best fits your garden:

A Install wire cable between two trees at least 8 ft. (2.4 m) high. Use chafe-protecting covers on the looped, attached ends. Avoid attachments that cut or penetrate bark. Hang plants or feeders from cable.

B Hang a support cable under a sturdy limb, protecting the tree by using a chafe protector where the cable contacts the bark. Use it to hang plants or feeders from the cable.

ARTIFICIAL NECTAR

Make your own nectar solution, following these guidelines to keep hummingbirds healthy. Use 1 part granulated sugar mixed with 4 parts hot, sterile water—either boiled or distilled. Avoid honey, brown sugar, or food coloring. Cover and cool the solution, fill the feeder, and refrigerate any remaining portion. Clean the feeder once a week substituting hot water and vinegar for soap.

C A simple 4×4 (89×89-mm) wood post, equipped with dowels and L-bracket shelves, will support both hanging plants and bird feeders.

D Fasten an eyebolt to an eave rafter or joist by drilling a hole through them. It will support even heavy plants or feeders. Brackets also can be attached to masonry.

E Stand-alone shade structures also can support hanging plants. Always evenly distribute each plant's weight on the structure.

PLANTING DEEP-THROATED FLOWERS

T rumpet-shaped flowers that contain nectar are the best source of food for hummingbirds—bountiful in supply, always fresh, and full of the exact nutrients the birds need. The best flowers to plant are those with vining habits; provide them tall supports, and they will sport dozens of blossoms on each plant [see Encyclopedia of Popular Bird and Butterfly Plants, pg. 95]. Gather your plants or seed, shovel, hand trowel, fertilizer, and gloves, then follow these easy steps:

1 Before you plant, install vertical poles or trellises to support the new vining plants.

2 For plants in nursery containers, dig a hole as deep as the container and half again as wide.

3 Add 0–10–10 fertilizer to soil in the planting hole at the package-recommended application rate. Mix thoroughly with a trowel.

4 Set the vine into the planting hole, backfill around it with soil, and firm the root area with your hands. Water.

5 To plant seed, check the package for proper planting depth and spacing for the species. Dig one or more furrows of proper depth, or plant in areas.

6 Plant seed in pairs at the recommended spacing. Loosely cover with soil, firm it with your open palms, and water using a spout with a diffusing rose.

HUMMINGBIRDS OF NORTH AMERICA TROCHILIDAE

Description	Range & Habitat	Attractive Plants
Allen's. *Selasphorus sasin.* Woodland hummingbird, to 3¾ in. (10 cm) long. Orange red; male has green back and crown, female indistinguishable from rufous.	Coastal California, Oregon. Casual to Arizona, New Mexico, Texas. Brush and woodland slopes.	Century plant, columbine, eucalyptus, fuchsia, cape honey-suckle, madrone, monkey-flower, nicotiana, Indian paintbrush, live oak, Monterey pine, coast redwood, scarlet sage.
Anna's. *Calypte anna.* Lowland hummingbird, to 4 in. (10 cm) long. Male has green back and red head, female green, gray with red-spotted throat.	Alaska, Arizona, coastal and central California, Oregon, Washington. British Columbia, Mexico. Brush, chaparral, desert, woodlands.	Coralbells, currant, eucalyptus, fuchsia, lion's-tail, nicotiana, penstemon, quince, sage.
Black-Chinned. *Archilochus alexandri.* Lowland hummingbird, to 3¾ in. (10 cm) long. Green, white; male has black throat, female has white breast, throat.	Desert and intermountain western North America. British Columbia, Mexico. Lowlands and foothills with brush, woodlands.	Garden balsam, canna, century plant, columbine, nicotiana, palo verde, shrimp plant, yucca.
Blue-Throated. *Lampornis clemenciae.* Streamside hummingbird, to 5 in. (13 cm) long. Green, blue, white; male has blue throat, tail, female has gray breast, throat.	Southern Arizona, New Mexico, Texas. Mexico. Casual north of range. Canyons, mountains, streams with brush, woodlands.	Garden balsam, canna, century plant, columbine, nicotiana, paloverde, shrimp plant, yucca.
Broad-Billed. *Cynanthus latirostris.* Desert hummingbird, to 4 in. (10 cm) long. Forked tail. Green, blue, white; male has blue throat, female has speckled breast, throat.	Southern Arizona, New Mexico, Texas. Mexico. Casual north of range. Canyons, mountains with brush, woodlands.	Cactus, century plant, columbine, nicotiana, ocotillo, poppy, yucca.
Broad-Tailed. *Selasphorus platycercus.* Woodland hummingbird, to 4 in. (10 cm) long. Green, white; male has red throat, female has tan or reddish breast, white throat.	Intermountain western North America. Mexico. Canyons, alpine meadows, woodlands.	Century plant, figwort, gilia, larkspur, lupine, nasturtium, ocotillo, penstemon, sage.
Calliope. *Stellula calliope.* Streamside hummingbird, to 3¼ in. (8 cm) long. Green, white; male has purple throat, female has tan breast, spotted cheek, throat.	Intermountain western North America. Canada. Alpine canyons, meadows, mountains, streams with wildflowers, woodlands.	Citrus, columbine, currant, monkey flower, penstemon, sage.
Costa's. *Calypte costae.* Desert hummingbird, to 3½ in. (9 cm) long. Green, white; male has purple throat, face; female has purple-spotted throat.	Southern Arizona, California. Mexico. Arroyos, canyons, chaparral, deserts with brush, cactus, wildflowers.	Bottlebrush, cactus, coralbells, eucalyptus, larkspur, nicotiana, ocotillo, sage, yucca.
Lucifer. *Callothorax lucifer.* Desert hummingbird, to 3½ in. (9 cm) long. White-tipped tail. Green, tan; male has purple throat; female has white throat.	Southern Arizona, New Mexico, Texas. Mexico. Casual north of range. Arroyos, canyons, chaparral, deserts, mountains with brush, cactus, wildflowers.	Cactus, century plant, columbine, nicotiana, ocotillo, poppy, yucca.
Magnificent (Rivoli's). *Eugenes fulgens.* Mountain hummingbird, to 5¼ in. (13 cm) long. Notched tail. Green, brown; male has green throat; female has white-spotted throat.	Southern Arizona, New Mexico. Mexico. Casual north of range. High desert canyons, mountains, streams with cactus, wildflowers.	Century plant, columbine, geranium, honeysuckle, penstemon, sage.
Ruby-Throated. *Archilochus colubris.* Woodland hummingbird, to 3¾ in. (10 cm) long. Green, white; male has red throat; female has white-spotted throat.	Eastern and midwest North America. Mexico. Brush and woodlands, surburban and urban gardens.	Beebalm, red buckeye, columbine, gladiolus, honeysuckle, mimosa, nasturtium.
Rufous. *Selasphorus rufus.* Woodland hummingbird, to 3¾ in. (10 cm) long. Red, green, white; male has flecked red plumage; female has red-spotted throat.	Pacific Northwest. British Columbia. Lowlands and mountains with brush, woodlands.	Abutilon, beebalm, columbine, currant, fuchsia, cape honey-suckle, larkspur, Indian paintbrush, penstemon.
Violet-Crowned. *Amazilia violiceps.* Streamside hummingbird, to 4½ in. (11 cm) long. Red bill. Green, white; both sexes have purple crown, white breast.	Southern Arizona, New Mexico. Mexico. Casual in Texas. Arroyos, canyons, streams with woodlands.	Mesquite, oak, ocotillo, poppy, sycamore.

OBSERVING HUMMINGBIRDS

When you plant flowers with nectar, bright colors—especially red—and tubular shapes, you're bound to have hummingbird visitors. Make sure your nectar supply is constant by planting species with overlapping bloom times, succeeding blooms, and long bloom cycles. You'll need a spot with some space around it and good visibility, so you easily can view the birds while preserving their privacy and safety. As with most wildlife, the best viewing occurs when you remain still and are some distance from the feeding or nesting area. Over time, you can approach closer to the birds as they become accustomed to your presence. You might be surprised at how close hummingbirds will allow you to approach.

Hummingbirds migrate in groups of separate sexes, with the males arriving first in their breeding areas. You'll be sure to notice them. Males of each species have much more brilliant plumage than the females' muted colorations. They select a perch with a good view, watching for the arrival of females. Each male chooses a territory and defends it with aggressive behavior and various unmusical calls. Courtship is very showy, with much swooping, and it takes place over an extended time, perhaps as long as a month. Then the male flies off to start another family. The female builds the nest, lays the tiny eggs, and raises the hatchlings.

While you'll usually see hummingbirds during the breeding season, those who live in a mild-winter climate can have visitors throughout the year. It's especially true if you hang a feeder during the coolest months [see Installing Hanging Feeders and Plants, pg. 75]. Keep in mind that other food sources may be scarce at this time of year, and the hummingbirds may come to depend on your feeder. Keep it stocked with nutritious nectar.

Many species of hummingbirds bear superficial resemblance to one another. Anna's, black-chinned, Costa's, juvenile ruby-throated, and any number of tropical hummingbird species bear iridescent green plumage. Consult a field guide with detailed pictures and observe the birds closely to identify them.

You're in for a great treat if you try to identify the visiting species. A field guide to species is useful, and several electronic sources also have information that can help you with identification [see On-Line, pg. 118]. In the eastern portion of North America, with only one common species—the ruby-throated hummingbird—it's easy. But in the west, from Texas to California and north along the Pacific coast, you'll see a dozen or so different types if you observe closely. Among these are Anna's, broad-tailed, calliope, Costa's and rufous hummingbirds.

As you watch, keep records for future reference and to share with friends. As with other wildlife species, patience and stillness are virtues that will reward you with displays of surprising beauty. Use the sound of the birds' distinctive wing-beat to help you locate them until you learn their preferred perches and feeding locations. If you wish to take photographs of the hummingbirds, as they feed, choose a very fast film, use a camera equipped with a telephoto lens, an electronic flash, and set the camera with very short shutter exposures to freeze them in flight. Even then, the incredibly fast wing beats still may be a blur.

ADAPTING A WINDOW TO WATCH HUMMINGBIRDS

Hummingbirds quickly adapt to human presence. Growing plants, hanging nectar feeders, and providing perches in a sunny spot near a window will provide hours of enjoyment in watching the birds. A simple modification will help you approach close to the feeding birds. Gather tinted window film, scissors, a sharp knife, bucket, squeegee, and gloves, then follow these steps:

1 Dark-tint film in rolls and sheets attached to backing paper is available at hardware and glass stores. Cut it to fit your window.

2 Thoroughly clean and dry the glass surface, using water and liquid detergent soap.

3 Follow the instructions that came with the tinted film for details on its application. Most films are applied to a moist window, but some are best rolled onto dry glass. Start at an edge. Using a squeegee, press it tightly to the glass.

4 Avoid trapping air bubbles as you apply the film. Peel the film back and reapply it as necessary to eliminate them.

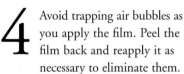

5 Use a razor knife to trim the film to the glass edges, using care to avoid damaging the frame or caulk.

6 The tinted film limits daytime visibility from outside the glass. Hang your feeder or trailing plants nearby, then observe from indoors.

ATTRACTING SONGBIRDS

A bird visitor that vocalizes with a series of musical tones is one of the sweetest rewards of your wildlife garden. Why do birds sing? They normally reserve their song for establishing territory and mating rituals, although some birds seem to sing for the sheer joy of it. When you offer consistent food and water supplies, your reward will be sightings of especially beautiful or occasional rare species, an eastern bluebird, perhaps, or an American goldfinch. By providing nesting sites, you ensure a greater number of visitors. Songbirds that are likely to visit include cardinals, chickadees, finches, nuthatches, orioles, robins, sparrows, swallows, swifts, tanagers, thrushes, titmice, towhees, warblers, and wrens.

Songbirds eat a widely varied diet. Some are carnivores that catch insects and worms; others are herbivores that eat seed, pollen, and buds; still others are omnivores, eating all these foods. Gardens that birds repeatedly visit must be diverse in their plantings. A landscape of freshly turned earth, planted with fruiting bushes, cosmos, roses, sunflowers, trees, and a few vines will ensure a year-round concert. Hang up a few feeders and install birdhouses with plenty of territory between them. A birdbath is another good addition.

Birds are a treat to the eye and ear, plus they're a boon in helping keep the insect, grub, and bug populations under control. On the other hand, you'll most likely also attract garden pests such as squirrels. You could plan to use squirrel-exclusionary methods when you choose feeders such as barrier hardware cloth or feeders that close when the weight of a squirrel tips the balance. For a last resort, you eventually even may resign yourself to separately feed the squirrels with a feeder of their own.

(Top) Trees that bloom in the early season will draw birds in spring to their brilliantly colored and scented blossoms.

(Above) Mountain chickadees are a common sight throughout the United States' and Canada's intermountain west.

(Right) Planting landscape trees provides perches for many types of birds. A juvenile warbler harvesting pollen-filled catkins and insects.

GROWING A BIRDHOUSE

Gourds with sturdy walls and hollow interiors have been used for centuries as birdhouses. A pair of vines will grow a dozen or more birdhouse gourds in a single garden season. Seed is available at garden stores and nurseries or from direct retailers. Gather your seed, hoe, watering can, gloves, and drill, then follow these easy steps:

1 Use your hoe to loosen the soil, incorporate any amendments or fertilizers, and raise a mound, 6–8 in. (15–20 cm) tall.

2 Build a watering moat by hoeing a ring of soil around the mound in a circle, 4–6 in. (10–15 cm) deep.

3 Note the planting depth recommended on the seed package. Atop the mound, use your finger to poke planting holes of that depth. Put two seeds in each hole and cover them with soil. Firm the soil.

4 Thoroughly water the planting. After the seeds sprout, fill the moat with water once or twice a week. The vines will grow, flower, and form gourds.

5 As the gourds mature, harvest the largest ones for birdhouses. Hang them in a warm, protected spot to dry.

6 Using a drill mounted with a 1 1/2-in. (38-mm) bit, cut a hole into the gourd. Remove all fiber and seeds. Mounting a 1/4-in. (6-mm) bit, drill a hole centered beneath the large opening.

7 Insert a 6-in. (15-cm) length of 1/4-in. (6-mm) dowel stock into the lower hole to make a perch. Attach a cup hook at the top. The birdhouse is ready to hang.

BIRDS ARE SPECIALIZED FEEDERS

Observing bird habits includes watching them eat and feeding their young. It's thrilling to observe as they carefully hunt worms, open pods, and crush seed coats. Because birds lack teeth, their food is ground together with fine stones and abrasive sand they carry in their crop. The shape and use of birds' bills differ from species to species.

The next time you are in your garden, examine some of the birds that perch in nearby trees or on fences. For a good look, use a pair of binoculars with moderate magnification and a wide field of view. Pay special attention to their bills and feet. You'll find that there are surprising variations between similar-appearing species, and soon you'll notice that those differences have a marked affect on their feeding behavior.

Bird's bills are shaped differently for specific feeding. Songbirds—chickadee and sparrow, for instance—are seed, grub, worm, and insect eaters. Their sharp, short, narrow, pointed bills enable them to pick seed out of a pod, grab an earthworm, or nab a crawling insect in a field of grass. Crossbills have interesting bills—the upper half curves in a different direction from the lower, enabling them to pluck seed from pinecones and other rather narrow crevices. The cardinal and grosbeak have short, wide, ratchet-type bills that permit them to crack acorns, small nuts, and large, hard-shelled seed. With a parrotlike, curved, and very strong bill, owls and falcons are able to catch, disable, and consume their scaled, feathered, or furred prey. Crows, jackdaws, magpies, ravens, and vultures have multipurpose bills suited to tearing carrion and crushing nuts or pits. The long, narrow bills of robins are ideal for quickly picking worms and grubs from loose soil. Regardless of birds' eating styles, their bills are also used to tote vast quantities of nest-building materials, for grooming, and to feed young birds still in the nest.

The more you look at birds in your garden, the more fascinating features you'll find—differences that extend beyond the colorful plumage they wear or the musical mastery found in their songs. To attract a specific bird species, note both its habits and the way it uses its specialized bill to obtain feed, then tailor aspects of your bird garden to its needs by providing the appropriate food and habitat.

Because bird species vary in the foods they consume, the garden that offers a smorgasbord—from crawling and burrowing insects to the rich, nutritious pollen of flowers—will host the widest variety of birds.

(Top to bottom) Finches crack tough seed, thrashers pick through fallen leaves, hummingbirds sip nectar, and woodpeckers pick insects from decaying wood.

WINTER FEEDING NEEDS

Offer natural feed such as sunflower heads, millet stalks, hard cracked corn, and seed mixtures. Suet —beef fat available in grocery meat sections —is another good choice to increase the caloric intake of some winter birds and encourage repeat visits. Place the suet in a mesh bag or smear it into knotholes in a section of timber. Hang it from a tree limb far enough off the ground to keep it out of the reach of household pets and any wildlife. Offer peanut butter and cut fruit but avoid bread, which could interfere with birds' natural digestion processes. Birds that particularly relish these foods are finches, nuthatches, and woodpeckers, among others. Keep feeders continuously stocked throughout the winter—once birds discover them, they'll depend on you for food. Discontinue offering suet once the weather warms.

FEEDING BIRDS

Winter Feeding Station

1 Wrap a log with hardware cloth. Using a hammer, drive roofing nails to hold the mesh in place. Trim any excess wire.

Birds that live in cold-winter climates need dependable, rich food such as seed containing oils and carbohydrates. Hang suet and seed feeders and grow seed-head-producing flowers to set out when temperatures plunge. To make your own suet feeder, you'll need a log, 4 inches (10 cm) wide and 18 inches (45 cm) long, plus hardware cloth with ¼-inch (6-mm) holes, roofing nails, a hammer, cup hook, and cord. To dry seed heads, you'll need string and an airy, warm, dry spot. Follow these steps:

2 Attach a hanger hook to the end of the log for a fastener. Tie a piece of stout cord to the hook.

3 Spread cooking lard or shortening on the feeder's wire with a putty knife. Coat the log by rolling it in birdseed.

4 Hang the filled feeder from a tree branch. As the birds eat seed and suet, refill the feeder.

Sunflower Seed Heads

1 After the petals drop, cut and hang the seed heads in an airy, warm, dry location for a few weeks to cure the seed.

2 Install a hanger in a tree or from an eave, using plastic-coated wire cable. A loop with a chafe-protecting sleeve made of garden hose is best.

3 Tie a seed head to the cable with twine looped under the head, then weight its dried stem to balance the head upright and provide easy access for the birds to eat seed.

COMMON SONGBIRDS OF NORTH AMERICA

Group and Family	Description	Selected Species
Blackbirds, Bobolink, Cowbirds, Grackles, Meadowlarks, Orioles, Tanagers. EMBERIZIDAE, ICTERIDAE, THRAUPIDAE. 23 species.	Black, brown, orange, purple, violet, yellow, highly patterned plumage, often with distinct color patches, collars, or wing flashes. Strong, swift flight. Sharply pointed bills used for berries, insects, nuts, seed. Widely ranging, varied habitats. Calls range from melodic to burrs, clicks, squeaks. Widespread distribution.	**Blackbirds:** Brewer's, *Euphagus cyanocephalus;* red-winged, *Agelaius phoeniceus;* rusty, *Euphagus carolinus;* yellow-headed, *Xanthocephalus xanthocephalus.* **Bobolink:** *Dolichonyx oryzivorus.* **Cowbirds:** bronzed, *Molothrus aenus;* brown-headed, *Molothrus ater.* **Grackles:** boat-tailed, *Quiscalus major;* common, *Quiscalus quiscula;* great-tailed, *Quiscalus mexicanus.* **Meadowlarks:** eastern, *Sturnella magna;* western, *Sturnella neglecta.* **Orioles:** hooded, *Icterus cucullatus;* northern, *Icterus galbula;* orchard, *Icterus spurius;* Scott's, *Icterus parisorum.* **Tanagers:** hepatic, *Piranga flava;* scarlet, *Piranga olivacea;* summer, *Piranga rubra;* western, *Piranga ludvociana.*
Buntings, Cardinals, Dickcissel, Grosbeaks. CARDINALINAE. 12 species. *noted grosbeak species are members of the FRINGILLIDAE family.	Showy or muted, brown, black, orange, red, yellow, highly patterned plumage, often with distinct color patches, breast markings, wing flashes, or crests. Conical, seed-cracking bills are canary-like (buntings, cardinals) or large, thick (grosbeaks). Melodic calls. Widespread distribution.	**Buntings:** indigo, *Passerina cyanea;* lark, *Calamospiza melanocorys;* lazuli, *Passerina amoena;* painted, *Passerina ciris;* snow, *Plectrophenax nivalis.* **Cardinals:** northern, *Cardinalis cardinalis;* pyrrhuloxia, *Cardinalis sinuatus.* **Dickcissel:** *Spiza americana.* **Grosbeaks:** black-headed, *Pheucticus melanocephalus;* blue, *Guiraca caerulea;* evening*, *Coccothraustes vespertinus;* pine*, *pinicola enucleator;* rose-breasted, *Pheucticus ludovicianus.*
Catbird, Mockingbird, Thrashers. MIMIDAE. Mimic thrushes. 10 species.	Generally muted, black, brown, gray-patterned plumage, some with gray, white-spotted breasts. Long, often curved, tactile bills used for berries, insects, seed. May prey on young of other bird species. Most varied and melodic of all North American songbirds, especially during mating season in late spring. Thrashers use their curved bills to till fallen leaves for insects.	**Catbird:** gray, *Dumetella carolinensis.* **Mockingbird:** northern, *Mimus polyglottos.* **Thrashers:** Bendire's, *Toxostoma bendirei;* brown, *Toxostoma rufum;* California, *Toxostoma redivivum;* crissal, *Toxostoma crissale;* curve-billed, *Toxostoma curvirostre;* Le Conte's, *Toxostoma lecontei;* long-billed, *Toxostoma longirostre;* sage, *Oreoscoptes montanus.*
Chickadees, Titmice. PARIDAE. 10 species.	Black, brown, gray, white, highly patterned plumage, lighter beneath, often with breast and chest markings, face flashes, and crests. Short bills used for seed, insects. Small birds with short wings, active foragers in woodlands. Melodic repeated calls. Widespread distribution.	**Chickadees:** black-capped, *Parus atricapillus;* boreal, *Parus hudsonicus;* Carolina, *Parus carolinensis;* chestnut-backed, *Parus rufescens;* Mexican, *Parus sclateri;* mountain, *Parus gambeli.* **Titmice:** bridled, *Parus wollweberi;* plain, *Parus inornatus;* tufted, *Parus bicolor.*
Dipper. CINCLIDAE. 1 species.	Muted dark gray with black gray head and lighter breast plumage. Medium-length, pointed bills used for aquatic insects. Very active in streams, woodlands. Wrenlike, melodic call. Strong underwater swimmers. Intermountain and coastal western North America.	American dipper, *Cinclus mexicanus.*
Finches, Goldfinches. FRINGILLIDAE (PASSERIDAE). 8 species.	Bright brown, gold, green, orange, red, rose, yellow-patterned plumage, often with distinct color patches, breast markings, and wing flashes. Short, strong bills used for seed. Migratory. Very melodic trills, tinkles, rolling scale calls. Widespread distribution.	**Finches:** Cassin's, *Carpodacus cassinii;* common rosefinch, *Carpodacus erythrinus;* house, *Carpodacus mexicanus;* purple, *Carpodacus purpureus;* rosy, *Leucosticte arctoa.* **Goldfinches:** American, *Carduelis tristis;* Lawrence's, *Carduelis lawrencei;* lesser, *Carduelis psaltria.*
Flycatchers, Kingbirds, Kiskadee, Pewee, Phoebe. TYRANNIDAE. Tyrant flycatchers. 33 species.	Mostly brown, gray-patterned plumage above, pink, rose, white breast, often with distinct color patches, collars, breast markings, and with whiskerlike face feathers. Broad, medium-length bills used for insects. Calls include clicks, trills, and *pip-pip-pip, dzeet, wit-will-doo* sounds.	**Flycatchers:** Acadian, *Empidonax virescens;* ash-throated, *Myiarchus cinerascens;* great crested, *Myiarchus crinitus;* olive-sided, *Contopus borealis;* scissor-tailed, *Tyrannus forficatus;* vermilion, *Pyrochephalus rubinus;* willow, *Empidonax traillii.* **Kingbirds:** eastern, *Tyrannus tyrannus;* thick-billed, *Tyrannus crassirostris;* western, *Tyrannus verticalis.* **Kiskadee:** great, *Pitangus sulphuratus.* **Pewee:** eastern, *Contopus virens;* olive-sided, *Contopus borealis;* western wood, *Contopus sordidulus.* **Phoebe:** eastern, *Sayornis phoebe.*
Gnatcatchers, Kinglets. MUSCICAPIDAE subfamily SYLVIINAE. Members of greater thrush family. 4 species.	**Gnatcatchers:** blue gray above, gray white beneath, with black tail and crown. **Kinglets:** olive gray above, yellow on breast, with black, red, yellow-striped crown. Tiny, round. Melodic trills, mews, and scolding, *jeh-dit* sounds.	**Gnatcatchers:** black-tailed, *Polioptila melanura;* blue-gray, *Polioptila caerulea.* **Kinglets:** golden-crowned, *Regulus satrapa;* ruby-crowned, *Regulus calendula.*

Group and Family	Description	Selected Species
Juncos, Longspurs, Sparrows, Towhees. EMBERIZIDAE. 40 species.	Varied black, brown, gray, red-patterned plumage above, lighter beneath, often with distinctive crowns, flashes, patches, and throat markings. Small, active. Short, conical bills used for berries, insects, seed. Calls include chirps, trills, whistles. Widespread, diverse distribution.	**Juncos:** dark-eyed, *Junco hyemalis;* yellow-eyed, *Junco phaeonotus.* **Longspurs:** chestnut-collared, *Calcarius ornatus;* McCown's, *Calcarius mccownii;* Smith's, *Calcarius pictus;* Lapland, *Calcarius lapponicus.* **Sparrows:** American tree, *Spizella arborea;* chipping, *Spizella passerina;* field, *Spizella pusilla;* lark, *Chondestes grammacus;* sage, *Amphispiza belli;* Savannah, *Passerculus sandwichensis;* song, *Melospiza melodia;* vesper, *Pooecetes gramineus.* **Towhees:** green-tailed, *Pipilo chlorurus;* rufous-sided, *Pipilo erythrophthalms.*
Martin, Swallows. HIRUNDINIDAE. 8 species.	**Martin:** blue purple plumage, gray beneath on female. Long, narrow, aerodynamic. Short-curved bill used for catching flying insects. **Swallows:** blue, brown, green, red plumage, lighter beneath. Short bill used for catching flying insects. Both types are long-distance migratory.	**Martin:** purple, *Progne subis.* **Swallows:** bank, *Riparia riparia;* barn, *Hirundo rustica;* cliff, *Hirundo pyrrhonata;* northern rough-winged, *Stelgidopteryx serripennis,* tree, *Tachycineta bicolor;* violet-green, *Tachycineta thalassina.*
Nuthatches. SITTIDAE. 4 species.	Black, blue, brown, gray-patterned plumage above, orange, tan, white beneath, with distinctive black or brown crown and white cheek markings. Small, very active. Medium-length, sharp bill used for picking insects from bark. Calls include *yank, wee-bee, bit-bit-bit* sounds. Widespread distribution.	Brown-headed, *Sitta pusilla;* pygmy, *Sitta pygmaea;* red-breasted, *Sitta canadensis;* white-breasted, *Sitta carolinensis.*
Starling. STURNIDAE. 1 introduced species.	Black, brown, green, white patterned plumage above, spotted breast; male mating plumage is iridescent purple black. Midsized, gregarious, active. Long, sharp bill used for berries, insects. Widespread distribution.	European, *Sturnus vulgaris.*
Thrushes, including Bluebirds, Robin. MUSCICAPIDAE subfamily TURDINAE. 10 species.	**Thrushes:** reddish brown plumage above, spotted white or red beneath, often with distinctive collar markings. **Bluebirds:** bright blue plumage above, light blue or cinnamon breast. **Robin:** Gray brown above, red or mottled breast. Midsized, active. Long, sharp bill used for insects. Migratory. Widespread distribution.	**Thrushes:** hermit, *Catharus guttatus,* Swainson's, *Catharus ustulatus;* Townsend's solitaire, *Myadestes townsendi;* varied, *Ixoreus naevius;* wood, *Hylocichla mustelina.* **Bluebirds:** eastern, *Sialia sialis;* mountain, *Sialia currucoides;* western, *Sialia mexicana.* **Robin:** American, *Turdus migratorius.*
Waxwings. BOMBYCILLIDAE. 2 species.	Reddish brown, gray above, tan gray, yellow beneath, with distinctive black, red, white, yellow wing flashes and raked crest. Midsized, gregarious, active. Short, wide bill used for berries, fruit. Migratory. Widespread distribution. Calls include buzzes, whistles.	Bohemian, *Bombycilla garrulus;* cedar, *Bombycilla cedrorum.*
Weavers, including Crossbills, Redpolls, House Sparrow, Siskin. PASSERIDAE. 6 species.	Bright brown, gold, green, orange, yellow, red, rose-patterned plumage, often with distinct color patches, breast markings, and wing flashes. Short, strong, sometimes crossing bills used for seed. Migratory, some with far-northern ranges. Very melodic trills, tinkles, rolling scale calls. Widespread distribution.	**Crossbills:** red, *Loxia curvirostra;* white-winged, *Loxia leucoptera.* **Redpolls:** common, *Carduelis flammea;* hoary, *Carduelis hornemanni.* **House Sparrow:** *Passer domesticus.* **Siskin:** pine, *Carduelis pinus.*
Wrens. TROGLODYTIDAE. 9 species.	Solid or patterned, brown, gray above, lighter beneath. Distinctive pointed tail. Tiny, very active. Long, curved, pointed bill used for insects, juniper berries. Migratory. Melodic buzzes, trills, chirps, warbling calls.	Bewick's, *Thryomanes bewickii;* cactus, *Campylorhynchus brunneicapillus;* canyon, *Catherpes mexicanus;* Carolina, *Thryothorus ludovicianus;* house, *Troglodytes aedon;* marsh, *Cistothorus palustris;* rock, *Salpinctes obsoletus;* sedge, *Cistothorus platensis;* winter, *Troglodytes troglodytes.*
Wood Warblers. EMBERIZIDAE subfamily PARULINAE 42 species.	Black, brown, orange, purple, violet, yellow, highly patterned plumage above, mostly yellow below, with distinct color patches. Sharply pointed bills used for berries, insects, seed. Streamside habitats. Calls range from melodic to burrs, squeaks and *szweet, bee-bzz-bzz.* Widespread distribution.	Black-and-white, *Mniotilta varia;* blackburnian, *Dendroica fusca;* black-throated gray, *Dendroica nigrescens;* Canada, *Wilsonia canadensis;* cerulean, *Dendroica cerulea;* Kentucky, *Oporornis formosus;* palm, *Dendroica palmarum;* pine, *Dendroica pinus;* prairie, *Dendroica discolor;* orange-crowned, *Vermivora celata;* worm-eating, *Helmitheros vermivorus;* yellow, *Dendroica petechia;* yellow-rumped, *Dendroica coronata;* yellow-throated, *Dendroica dominica.*

OBSERVING SONGBIRDS

Once you've invited winged visitors into your garden, plan time in your day to watch them. You'll first notice their habits. Cardinals feed at morning and evening, for example, while mourning doves usually feed during the day. Although plants will provide the birds' main food sources, you should add a bird feeder or two to your landscape. Place them at varying heights, and keep them filled.

Soon after the garden is blooming and your feeders are in place, avoid the area and give the birds privacy. The birds soon will discover the food. Because songbirds are more wary than hummingbirds, they quickly fly away when disturbed. You'll need two essential skills: patience and stillness. After the birds have been feeding undisturbed for some time, opportunities will come for you to gradually reveal your presence. Move slowly and they soon will adjust to your presence.

If your garden includes a water feature, you'll be able to watch the birds drinking and bathing. In areas safe from predators, some birds will sun themselves on the ground, while others may take dust baths.

Bird-watching is a pastime enjoyed by nature lovers from every walk of life. Besides the pleasure of fresh air and sunshine, those who take up bird-watching as a hobby surround themselves with flowers as well as the beautifully marked winged creatures they observe.

Encourage nesting in spring by hanging mesh bags—the sort in which onions are packaged—filled with bits of string, straw, dryer lint, even pet hair, for birds to use for nest building. In a landscape with a variety of tree and shrub species, several species are likely to nest. Robins, for example, often nest in lilac or medium-sized holly trees. By planting either type of shrub near a window, you'll have a good view when birds are sitting on the nest and after chicks have hatched. You'll be able to watch the young birds as they eat, grow, gain confidence, and eventually fly away.

You easily can view songbirds in the landscape from your indoor location, preserving the birds' sense of privacy. Use binoculars to see the details of bird plumage or a camera mounted with a telephoto lens to help preserve the moment. A field guide will help you identify new birds. In a large landscape, construct a blind to provide you with cover to closely observe your bird garden [see Building a Small Backyard Blind, next pg.]. After some time, you'll become familiar with certain species and, perhaps, even with some individual birds.

BUILDING A SMALL BACKYARD BLIND

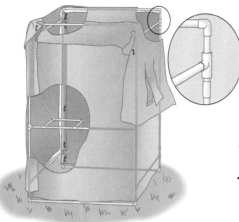

Blinds are useful for closely observing or photographing backyard birds, and are simple to construct and use. The blind shown here is easily assembled with porous shade fabric draped over a PVC-pipe frame. Add a comfortable chair, and allow the birds to become accustomed to the blind for a few days before first use. Gather the necessary materials and follow these steps:

1 Make eight joints by sliding a reduction tee over a ¾×5-in. (19×127-mm) piece of PVC pipe between an el and a straight fitting.

2 Use the joints from step 1 to assemble the two side frames, using two uprights and two crossbars to make each frame rectangle.

3 Use a reduction bushing fitted to a crossbrace to connect the two side frames. Frame a basket bar with four tees, two els, and spare pipe.

4 Horizontally wrap one length of shade fabric around the blind. Fold the corners and fasten it with pins. Then drape the second piece over the top.

Required Materials:

From ¾-in. (19-mm) Schedule 40 PVC PIPE:

4	6-ft. (1.8-m)	Uprights
	(Two cut at 2 ft. (60 cm) to fit basket shelf frame)	
4	5-ft. (1.5-m)	Crossbars
1	40-in. (102-cm)	Basket Bar
	(Cut at 2 ft. (60 cm) to fit basket shelf frame)	
4	4-ft. (1.2-m)	Crossbraces
10	¾-in. (19-mm)	S-S 90° El Fittings
4	¾-in. (19-mm)	S-S-S Tee Fittings
8	¾-in. (19-mm)	S-S Straight Fittings
8	1×¾-in. (25×19-mm)	S-S-S Reduction Tees
8	1×¾-in. (25×19-mm)	S-S Reduction Bushings

Other Components:

2	6-ft (1.8 m)	60% Green shade fabric
	(5 ft. (1.5 m) wide)	
25	1-in. (25-mm)	Stainless safety pins

5 At seated eye level, carefully cut a moveable viewing flap out of the front panel, leaving it attached at the top.

6 To use the blind, seat yourself in a chair. Use the basket to hold binoculars, a field guide, and other items.

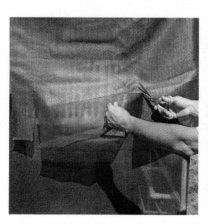

ATTRACTING MIGRATORY BIRDS

On their way to nesting or wintering areas, a flock of robins, red-eyed vireos, or other colorful or unusual birds may stop in your garden. Migratory birds visit seasonally according to their own natural and internal schedules. There are four major north-south migration routes—flyways—over North America, plus many smaller, local corridors. Similar flyways are located in most parts of the world. The Pacific flyway runs along the west coast from Canada and the Arctic to Central America. The central flyway and the Mississippi flyway intersect at certain broad locations in mid-continent as they follow generally North-South routes. The Atlantic flyway, which follows the east coast, has many branches, with a main artery originating in Canada's Arctic Quebec.

Many birds migrate to some degree. Some North American species you may see include red-winged blackbird, bluebird, bunting, chickadee, cowbird, creeper, crow, dickcissel, dove, finch, grackle, grosbeak, hawk, hummingbird, jay, junco, mockingbird, nuthatch, oriole, redpoll, robin, siskin, sparrow, starling, tanager, brown thrasher, thrush, towhee, warbler, woodpecker, and wren. The birds' timing and length of stay will vary, depending on whether the visitor is there to winter through the season, avoid cold highland temperatures, nest and rear young, or take advantage of the balmy summer weather in your region.

THE MIGRATION MIRACLE

Size is a poor predictor of migratory ability and distance; birds as small as the hummingbird—3 inches (75 mm) long—and as large as the whooping crane—5 feet (1.5 m) tall—both migrate and have vast ranges. Some birds travel long distances twice a year, following the sun as the seasons change.

Birds that prefer cool, wet zones generally fly from the middle latitudes toward the poles as spring progresses; in autumn, they return to more temperate areas. Others fly from continent to continent or hemisphere to hemisphere in search of ideal climate and food.

How do they do it? Some such as pigeons sense magnetic fields of the earth, while others—Canada geese, as an example—follow experienced lead birds. And, other birds migrate with instincts that behaviorists have yet to unravel.

A female American goldfinch has more subdued plumage than the brightly colored males. All are found in deciduous forests and grassy fields; to draw them to your yard, plant fruit trees, seed-filled grasses, and thistles.

If your garden is in one of the general flyways, you're sure to see some transients if you offer consistent supplies of water and food. Migratory birds often are hungry and need to build up their fat reserves for further migration. Using keen eyesight, they'll see your scattered cracked corn, sunflower seed, and millet. Offer it in early autumn, repeating in early spring for the returning travelers. Keep the area free of predators. Consider constructing a bird blind [see Building a Small Backyard Blind, previous pg.].

MIGRATORY ROUTES OF COMMON SONGBIRDS

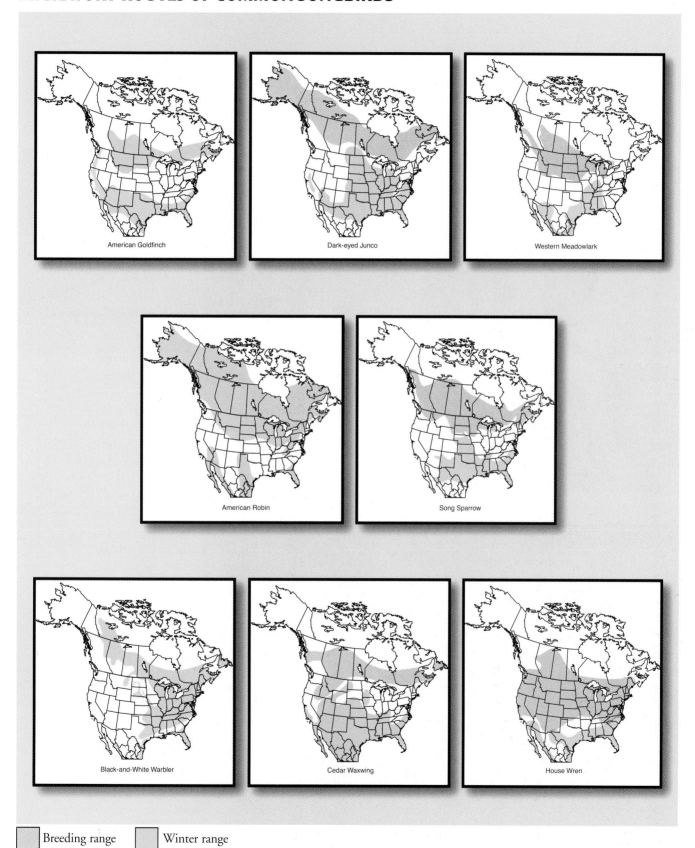

Breeding range   Winter range

OTHER COLORFUL BIRDS

(Right) The California quail is a frequent vistor to backyards that margin on wildlands.

(Below) A yellow-billed magpie is more rarely seen than its black-billed cousins that are a common sight in the mountain northwest, British Columbia, and Alaska.

(Bottom) You'll recognize the ground-nesting killdeer by its unique and ear-piercing call of "kill-dee-dee-dee.

Many other varieties of birds are occasional visitors to backyard gardens. With a field guide and your life list in hand and a pair of binoculars, watch for these colorful and interesting birds that may visit your yard:

Crows, starlings, cowbirds, and grackles: Sometimes considered coarse and raucous, these birds have a gregarious nature, interesting plumage and markings, and habits. Some species lay their eggs in the nests of other birds, leaving the foster parents to rear their young.

Doves and pigeons: Quiet, somewhat wary birds, doves and pigeons mainly are ground feeders. You'll find them eating millet seed spilled from feeders or dusting their feathers.

Game birds: Grouse, partridge, pheasant, and quail visit vegetable gardens, fallow fields, and meadows. They'll dust themselves when provided a site and will ingest small stones to help them digest insects and seed.

Jays: Bright-colored characters add action and sound to the garden. Keep them from cleaning out your songbird feeders by providing them one of their own filled with sunflower seed and peanuts.

Owls and raptors: In areas of woodland, fields, and hills, hawks circle overhead. Owls may visit as well; you can hear owls' calls in the evening—a great horned owl duet is an unforgettable concert. Large birds of prey nest in tall evergreens, deciduous trees, large airy barns, or roosting boxes set high in a tree.

Roadrunners: A cuckoo relative, this unusual bird of arid regions is more likely to run at great speed than fly, roosts in dead trees, and eats reptiles.

Waterfowl: Depending on proximity to wetlands and shores, you may see such water birds as avocet, coot, cormorant, duck, egret, flamingo, godwit, goose, gull, heron, killdeer, kingfisher, kittiwake, pelican, phalarope, plover, rail, sanderling, sandpiper, snipe, spoonbill, stilt, stint, tern, and woodcock. Most are best watched at a distance.

Woodpeckers: These delightful birds range from tiny to quite large, visiting even small city gardens. Their diet of termites and other insects inhabiting rotting wood make them carnivores, but some species also eat acorns, nuts, and seed.

OTHER BIRDS OF NORTH AMERICA

Group and Family	Description	Selected Species
Anis, Cuckoos. CUCULIDAE. Anis, 2 species; cuckoos, 3 species; roadrunner, 1 species.	**Anis:** black, stout, crowlike with large bill, ruffled plumage. **Cuckoos:** brown, tan and white, sleek and raptorlike. **Roadrunners:** colorfully plumaged and long-tailed. Carnivorous. Calls range from monotonous repeated *cu-cu-cu* or *gaw-gaw-gaw* to dovelike cooing or clicking.	**Anis:** groove-billed ani, *Crotophaga sulcirostris;* smooth-billed ani, *Crotophaga ani.* **Cuckoos:** black-billed cuckoo, *Coccyzus erythropthalmus;* yellow-billed cuckoo, *Coccyzus americanus.* **Roadrunners:** greater roadrunner, *Geococcyx californianus.*
Crows, Jays, Magpies, Ravens. CORVIDAE. Crows, 3 species; jays, 6 species; magpies, 2 species; nutcracker, 1 species; ravens, 2 species.	**Crows:** large, heavy billed, and black. **Jays:** blue, gray, sometimes with topnotches. **Magpies:** black and white patterned with irridescent green wing plumage. **Nutcracker:** gulllike in appearance. **Ravens:** the largest of the group, with black plumage. All have loud, raucous calls.	**Crows:** American, *Corvus brachyrhynchos;* fish, *Corvus ossifragus;* northwestern, *Corvus caurinus.* **Jays:** blue, *Cyanocitta cristata;* gray, *Perisoreus canadensis;* pinyon, *Gymnorhinus cyanocephalus;* scrub, *Aphelocoma coerulescens.* **Magpies:** black-billed, *Pica pica;* yellow-billed, *Pica nuttalli.* **Nutcracker:** Clark's, *Nucifraga columbiana.* **Ravens:** common, *Corvus corax.*
Grouse, Ptarmigans. PHASIANIDAE. Bobwhite, 1 species; chukar, 1 introduced species; grouse, 5 species; partridge, 1 introduced species; pheasant, 1 introduced species; prairie chicken, 2 species; ptarmigan, 3 species; quail, 5 species; turkey, 1 species.	**Bobwhite:** reddish brown, patterned, quaillike. **Chukar:** black, brown, gray patterned, stocky. **Grouse:** brown, red, white patterned, fan-tailed. **Partridge:** brown, gray, red patterned, large. **Pheasant:** brown, iridescent green, red patterned, very large. **Prairie chicken:** distinctive ruff and red, yellow eye combs, distinctive *oo-loo-who* call. **Ptarmigan:** brown patterned turning white, seasonally phased plumage. **Quail:** brown, gray, marked plumage, with distinctive plume. **Turkey:** largest gamebird, with red, white wattles and iridescent brown, green, red plumage.	**Bobwhite:** northern, *Colinus virginianus.* **Grouse:** blue, *Dendragapus obscurus;* ruffed, *Bonasa umbellus;* sage, *Centrocercus urophasianus;* spruce, *Dendragapus canadensis.* **Pheasant:** ring-necked, *Phasianus colchicus.* **Prairie chicken:** greater, *Tympanuchus cupido;* lesser, *Tympanuchus pallidicinctus.* **Ptarmigan:** rock, *Lagopus mutus;* white-tailed, *Lagopus leucurus;* willow, *Lagopus lagopus.* **Quail:** California, *Callipepla californica;* Gambel's, *Callipepla gambelii;* mountain, *Oreortyx pictus;* scaled, *Callipepla squamata.* **Turkey:** wild, *Meleagris gallopavo.*
Owls. TYONIDAE, STRIGIDAE. Barn owl, 1 species; typical owls, 18 species.	**Barn owl:** reddish brown above, white-spotted underside, to 16 in. (41 cm) tall. **Typical owls:** depending on species, brown, reddish brown, brown, gray, red, some with white winter phases. All have immobile eyes in large heads, silent flight owing to soft, aerodynamic plumage. Calls include barking, hisses, hooting, screeches or *hooo, hoo-ahh, who-who-err-uuu* sounds.	**Barn owl:** *Tyto alba.* **Typical owls:** barred, *Strix varia;* boreal, *Aegolius funereus;* burrowing, *Athene cunicularia;* eastern screech, *Otus asio;* elf, *Micrathene whitneyi;* flammulated, *Otus flammeolus;* great gray, *Strix nebulosa;* great horned, *Bubo virginianus;* long-eared, *Asio otus;* northern hawk, *Surnia ulula;* northern pygmy, *Glaucidium gnoma;* northern saw-whet, *Aegolius acadicus;* short-eared, *Asio flammeus;* snowy, *Nyctea scandiaca;* spotted, *Strix occidentalis;* western screech, *Otus kennicottii;* whiskered screech, *Otus trichopsis.*
Pigeons, Doves. COLUMBIDAE. Pigeons, 3 species; doves, 6 species.	**Pigeons:** black, gray wings with gray, purple breast and head, neck cloaked in irridescent gray, green feathers. Varied markings. **Doves:** reddish brown, gray, red, tan, white, or white-tipped wings with cinnamon, violet, white breast and head. Narrow to stocky, aerodynamic bodies. Calls include *coo, up-cu-pah-coo, cuk-cuk-coo, ooh-hoo-ooh-hurrup,* among others.	**Pigeons:** band-tailed, *Columba fasciata;* red-billed, *Columba flavirostris;* white-crowned, *Columba leucocephala.* **Doves:** common ground, *Columbina passerina;* Inca, *Columbina inca;* mourning, *Zenaida macroura;* rock, *Columba livia;* white-winged, *Zenaida asiatica;* white-tipped, *Leptotila verreauxi.*
Shrikes. LANIIDAE. 2 species.	Black, brown wings with distinctive, mockingbird-like white flash with gray, tan head and black tail tipped in white, to 10 in. (25 cm) tall. Calls include low-toned warbles mixed with squeaks, screeches, or *shak-shak.*	Loggerhead, *Lanius ludovicianus;* northern, *Lanius excubitor.*
Swifts. APODIDAE. 4 species.	Brown, gray, tan wings with white, tan breast and neck, brown head. Very slender and aerodynamic body; 4¾–7 in. (12–18 cm) long; narrow, long wings. Summers; migrates great distances.	Black, *Cypseloides niger;* chimney, *Chaetura pelagica;* Vaux's, *Chaetura vauxi;* white-throated, *Aeronautes saxatalis.*
Woodpeckers, Flicker, Sapsuckers. PICIDAE. Woodpeckers, 16 species; flicker, 1 species; sapsuckers, 4 species.	**Woodpeckers:** brightly marked brown, black, yellow, spotted wings with gray, tan, white breast and black, white, red, yellow patterned heads. **Flicker:** similar to woodpeckers; black or red face stripe, distinctive crescent bib. **Sapsuckers:** similar to woodpeckers; yellow marked breast, patterned or solid brown, red head.	**Woodpeckers:** downy, *Picoides pubescens;* hairy, *Picoides villosus;* ladder-backed, *Picoides scalaris;* Lewis', *Melanerpes lewis;* Nuttall's, *Picoides nuttallii;* pileated, *Dryocopus pileatus;* red-bellied, *Melanerpes carolinus;* red-cockaded, *Picoides borealis;* red-headed, *Melanerpes erythrocephalus.* **Flicker:** northern, *Colaptes auratus.* **Sapsuckers:** red-naped, *Sphyrapicus nuchalis;* Williamson's, *Sphyrapicus thyroideus;* yellow-bellied, *Sphyrapicus varius.*

BIRD-WATCHING AND PHOTOGRAPHY

Good eyes and ears are all you need for enjoying birds and hummingbirds. For the most enjoyable watching, inform yourself about the birds you see. By observing carefully, you can train your eye to see more specific details. If you are new to bird-watching, learn what and where to look on the bird's body for their identifying details. Acquire a quality field guide to start a list of birds you've seen—a life list—and keep it up to date. Take notes on the dates that species are seen, the time of day, their activity, flowers in bloom, and other such details.

The secret to photographing all wildlife—birds, butterflies, insects, and mammals—is gaining a thorough knowledge of each subject's behaviorial patterns and habits. Learn the time of day that the birds feed along with likely locations in your garden, and you'll be able to take good photographs of them. If they display special colors during their mating season, take that fact into consideration. In time, you'll increase your ability to be ready with your equipment at the very moment your subject appears.

The reward for a careful, quiet wait is this portrait of a white-crowned sparrow foraging on the forest floor. Use a 35-mm or digital camera with a long telephoto or zoom lens mounted on a sturdy tripod, fast film, and your patience to take great birding photographs.

Taking photographs of birds and butterflies is a great way to keep records of your winged visitors. Make notes on your slides or prints, or put them in an organizer or use an album with room to note your comments by the photographs. Be patient—birds and other wildlife move frequently and quickly. To best photograph them, acquire a 35-mm or a digital camera equipped with a high-magnification zoom lens featuring close-up focusing, a solid tripod, and a fast print film of ISO 200–400. You'll also find it helpful to bring along your binoculars or a spotting scope to help you locate the subjects before moving your camera to another location or settling down for a long wait. Observe the new location for a few minutes, note the light and shadow areas, and the behavior of your subject.

Lenses longer than 300 mm—many bird photographers routinely use lenses over 500 mm—are prone to movement that blurs photographs. You can reduce this tendency by using a sturdy tripod and by setting your shutter speed to the fastest exposure possible for your light conditions. In a similar way, close-up photographs frequently are blurry unless they are taken with special lenses; fixed-focus cameras generally should be avoided for taking pictures of butterflies and birds. Close-ups taken in low-light conditions lack depth of field—an area of sharpness from front to back of the subject—and may seem blurry; use an electronic flash to add the necessary light needed to take steadier, sharper-appearing photographs.

Find advice or help through bird-watching or photography clubs, where you'll get pointers about catching your local wildlife on film. Visit nature centers and photography exhibits for inspiring examples of the craft. Begin keeping albums, either the old-fashioned paper kind or digital albums for sharing electronically with friends. If you have children, include them when bird-watching, and teach them how to take photographs of what they see. It's a wonderful family hobby.

BIRDING EQUIPMENT

Your eyes and ears are your best beginning equipment. As you become more curious when peering at your visitors through windows or from behind bushes, you may want a closer look. Some additional items may be a big help to you for studying details of birds and butterflies, or for taking photographs. Many nature lovers go on birding trips, and for these you may want some or all of the equipment listed here:

Binoculars: The very name means two fields of vision, translating to adjustable viewing for each eye. Binoculars are probably the most important piece of bird-viewing equipment. These optical enhancers are stamped with numbers such as 7×35. The first number is the magnification; the higher the number, the greater the apparent magnification and the closer the subject appears. The second number represents the diameter of the lenses in millimeters. The larger the lenses, the more light that comes through them and the easier it is to see the bird. There are standard as well as zoom binoculars and compact types, some of which are waterproof. Obtain the best binoculars you can afford, after an outdoor trial, and treat them as you would any other precision instrument.

Spotting scopes: These monovision aids are usually used on a tripod as a temporary stationary viewing location. They are also stamped with magnification and lens size. As you consider them, be sure you try each model outdoors until you find one that works best for you. Lightweight, compact pen scopes are also available.

Cameras: Depending on your level of interest, you can use anything from an inexpensive recyclable waterproof camera to a professional single-lens reflex or digital model with a 500-mm or longer telescopic lens. If you are very interested in photography, obtain a camera with an entire system of lenses and controls. Learn more about bird photography by researching books on the subject, visiting electronic information sources, and discussing your hobby with camera store staff.

Clothing: Waterproof shoes, boots, or waders are a good idea if your outdoor area is large and conditions are inclement; otherwise, neutral-colored trail wear is all that you'll need. Rip-stop trousers are a boon. A lightweight photographer's vest is handy for holding film, pencils, or your field guides.

Field guides: Reliable field guides are filled with excellent color illustrations, often showing various species by male and female, as well as immature and mature plumage. Peterson's guides and those of the Audubon Society are very helpful in teaching you how to identify birds—each species has clearly identifiable markings—which adds to your pleasure and can enrich your planning and planting for wildlife in the future.

Other gear: A backpack, top-loading film bag, extra-light tripod, and walking stick also may be helpful.

To obtain your equipment, consider photography and electronics retailers, nature hobby retailers, direct merchants, and electronic merchants as possible suppliers. Always check their business practices, repair service options, and the warranties they offer before you make your final selection.

Useful equipment for birding: a spotting scope or binoculars, log book or life list, field identification guides, and a camera.

Once you've learned you can plant specifically to attract birds, hummingbirds, and butterflies, consider the wide range of plant material available to you in creating your wildlife habitat. The plants listed on the following pages are categorized to help make it easy for you to choose at a glance the types of plants you prefer. You will find a selection of flowering plants, shrubs and small trees, and vines in three divided sections, listed in alphabetical order by common name. Scientific names are also given and are listed in the index. It's best to shop by the scientific name—genus and species— which is standard throughout the world. In some cases only the genus name is given, because many species of that genus are suited for the purpose. Most of these plants are easy to obtain from various sources, through local retail garden retailers or from direct plant merchants. The best choice and supply of plants is usually found at the beginning of the spring season. Obtain your plants early for the very best selection.

A selection of flowering plants, shrubs, trees, and vines for winged wildlife, plus their planting and care needs

Encyclopedia of Popular Bird and Butterfly Plants

As you read through the listed plants, you'll see that most which successfully attract birds, hummingbirds, and butterflies are quite common in gardens; many of them you already may have seen or even possibly grown. You can obtain a variety of plants from these lists, fully confident in the knowledge that you'll be making the right selections for your wildlife landscape.

Experts agree that the best wildlife habitat is one that is widely diversified. Therefore, choose some plants from each category. If yours is a new site, include several types of large trees for shelter and nesting areas. Choose several small trees to provide flowers, fruit, shelter, and nesting and perching areas. Select several species to group separately in the landscape, and at least one red, deep-throated flowering vine for hummingbirds. Among the perennials and annuals, you'll find all sorts of bright flowers as the finishing touches for your "red carpet" wildlife habitat. You are assured plenty of active enjoyment when you choose a balanced selection of plant materials for your wildlife visitors to enjoy.

(Clockwise from top left) Many plants that attract birds, hummingbirds, and butterflies include lovely flowers that you'll explore in the pages that follow: golden sunflower, ruby fuchsia, variegated foxglove, and heavenly blue morning glory.

FLOWERING PLANTS

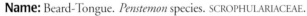

Name: Aster, China; Annual Aster. *Callistephus chinensis.* ASTERACEAE (COMPOSITAE).
Description: Upright or branching annual herb, 8–32 in. (20–80 cm) tall. Matte, green, oval or lance-shaped, deeply toothed leaves, to 5 in. (13 cm) long. Blue, pink, purple, red, white, yellow flowers, in early–late summer. Many cultivars are available.
Attracts: Birds, hummingbirds with flowers, nectar, seed.
Plant hardiness: Tender. Self-seeding, zones 6–10.
Site/Soil: Full–filtered sun. Moist, well-drained soil. Fertility: Rich. 6.5–7.0 pH.
Planting: Space 1 ft. (30 cm) apart after frost hazard has passed.
Care: Easy. Keep evenly moist; avoid wetting foliage. Fertilize monthly. Mulch. Deadhead spent flowers and pinch foliage to prolong bloom. Propagate by seed.
Features: Good choice for beds, containers. Good for cutting. Leafhopper and aster wilt, aster yellows susceptible; rotate plantings each year.

Name: Beard-Tongue. *Penstemon* species. SCROPHULARIACEAE.
Description: About 250 species of upright or rounded perennial herbs or woody shrubs, 2–3 ft. (60–90 cm) tall. Usually shiny, green, lance-shaped leaves, 2–4 in. (50–100 mm) long. Many pink, purple, red, white, bicolor with white, trumpet-shaped, flared flowers with delicately spotted throats, in spring–summer.
Attracts: Birds, butterflies, hummingbirds with insects, nectar, seed.
Plant hardiness: Varies by species, zones 3–10.
Site/Soil: Full sun–partial shade. Moist, very well-drained, sandy soil. Fertility: Average. 5.5–6.5 pH.
Planting: Space 12–18 in. (30–45 cm) apart after frost hazard has passed.
Care: Easy. Allow soil surface to dry between waterings. Fertilize monthly during active growth. Deadhead spent blossoms to prolong bloom. Protect from standing water, heat. Propagate by cuttings, division, seed.
Features: Good choice for color, beds, borders, edgings, fences, paths. Pest and disease resistant.

Name: Bee Balm; Oswego Tea. *Monarda didyma.* LAMIACEAE (LABIATAE).
Description: Bushy, upright perennial herb, to 4 ft. (1.2 m) tall. Fragrant, textured, mint green, oval to lance-shaped, toothed leaves, 3–6 in. (75–150 mm) long, with downy undersides. Single or double whorls of pink, scarlet, white, fluffy, tubular, double-lipped, irregular flowers, to 2 in. (50 mm) long, in summer.
Attracts: Bees, birds, butterflies, hummingbirds with flowers, nectar, insects.
Plant hardiness: Zones 4–9. Best in cold-winter climates.
Site/Soil: Partial shade. Moist, well-drained humus. Fertility: Average. 6.5–7.0 pH.
Planting: Space 2 ft. (60 cm) apart after soil warms.
Care: Easy. Keep evenly moist during active growth. Avoid fertilizing. Propagate by divisions, seed in spring.
Features: Good choice for backgrounds, borders, massed plantings. Powdery mildew, rust susceptible.

Name: Bellflower. *Campanula* species. CAMPANULACEAE.

Description: More than 300 species of mostly low, slender, leafy annual, biennial, or perennial herbs, 2–3 ft. (60–90 cm) tall. Shiny or textured, green, spear-shaped leaves, 4–8 in. (10–20 cm) long, with central flower stalks. Many blue, purple, white, cup-shaped flowers, to 1½ in. (38 mm) wide, in spring–autumn.

Attracts: Birds, hummingbirds with flowers, insects, nectar, seed.

Plant hardiness: Zones 3–10. Evergreen, zones 9–10.

Site/Soil: Full sun–partial shade. Damp, well-drained humus. Fertility: Average. 6.5–7.0 pH.

Planting: Space 12–18 in. (30–45 cm) apart after frost hazard has passed.

Care: Easy. Keep moist. Fertilize annually in spring. Divide in early spring or autumn when crowded. Propagate by cuttings, division, seeds.

Features: Good choice for beds, borders, ground cover. Good for cutting. Spider mite, slug, snail and aster yellows susceptible.

Name: Black-Eyed Susan; Coneflower; Gloriosa Daisy. *Rudbeckia hirta.* ASTERACEAE (COMPOSITAE).

Description: Tall, upright, branching, annual, biennial, or perennial herbs, 2–3 ft. (60–90 cm) tall. Textured, hairy, green, lance-shaped leaves, to 4 in. (10 cm) long. Showy, orange-yellow blend, daisylike flowers, 2–4 in. (50–100 mm) wide, with dark cone-shaped centers, in summer–autumn.

Attracts: Birds, butterflies with flowers, insects, seed.

Plant hardiness: Zones 3–10.

Site/Soil: Full sun–partial shade. Moist, well-drained soil. Fertility: Average. 6.0–7.5 pH.

Planting: Space 1 ft. (30 cm) apart after frost hazard has passed.

Care: Easy. Allow surface soil to dry between waterings. Deadhead spent flowers to prolong bloom. Divide perennials when crowded. Propagate by cuttings, division, seed.

Features: Good choice for backgrounds, borders, massed plantings. Good for cutting. Pest and disease resistant.

Name: Blanket Flower. *Gaillardia* species. ASTERACEAE (COMPOSITAE).

Description: About 14 species of bushy, upright, annual, biennial, or perennial herbs, 2–3 ft. (60–90 cm) tall. Alternate, hairy, textured, dark gray green, lance-shaped leaves, 3–6 in. (75–150 mm) long. Showy, gold, deep red tipped in yellow, or yellow flowers, 3–4 in. (75–100 mm) wide, with dark purple, yellow, or brown centers, in early summer–autumn.

Attracts: Birds, butterflies with flowers, seed.

Plant hardiness: Zones 3–9. Self-seeding, zones 5–9.

Site/Soil: Full sun. Damp–dry, well-drained, sandy humus. Fertility: Average–low. 6.0–7.5 pH.

Planting: Space 10–15 in. (25–38 cm) apart when soil is workable.

Care: Easy. Allow surface soil to dry between waterings. Stake taller cultivars. Avoid fertilizing. Deadhead spent flowers to promote bloom. Prune roots in summer. Divide when crowded in spring. Propagate by cuttings, division, seed.

Features: Good choice for beds, borders. Good for cutting. Aphid and leaf spot, powdery mildew susceptible.

Name: Cardinal Flower; Indian Pink. *Lobelia cardinalis.* CAMPANULACEAE.

Description: Upright, slender perennial herb, 2–4 ft. (60–120 cm) tall. Shiny, medium to dark green, oval to lance-shaped, finely toothed leaves, to 4 in. (10 cm) long. Many pink, red, white, spirelike flowers, 1–1½ in. (25–38 mm) wide, with drooping, honeysuckle-like lips, in late summer. Many different cultivars and hybrids available

Attracts: Birds, butterflies, hummingbirds with flowers, nectar, seed.

Plant hardiness: Zones 2–10.

Site/Soil: Full sun–partial shade. Very moist, well-drained humus. Fertility: Rich. 6.5–7.5 pH.

Planting: Space 1 ft. (30 cm) apart after frost hazard has passed.

Care: Moderate–challenging. Keep evenly moist. Fertilize annually in spring. Mulch. Propagate by cuttings, division, seed.

Features: Good choice for backgrounds, beds, borders, edgings, and water feature margins. Pest and disease resistant.

Name: Columbine. *Aquilegia* species. RANUNCULACEAE.

Description: About 70 species of graceful, upright, open perennials, 18–48 in. (45–120 cm) tall. Fine-textured, light silvery green leaves, in 2–3 lobed groups. Showy, blue, pink, white, yellow, and bicolored, cup-and-saucer-shaped flowers, 1½–4 in. (38–100 mm) wide and to 6 in. (15 cm) long, in early summer.

Attracts: Bees, birds, butterflies, hummingbirds with flowers, nectar.

Plant hardiness: Zones 3–10.

Site/Soil: Full sun–partial shade. Moist, very well-drained sandy humus. Fertility: Rich–average. 6.5–7.5 pH.

Planting: Space 1–2 ft. (30–60 cm) apart after soil warms.

Care: Easy. Keep moist during active growth; reduce watering after flowers fade. Fertilize semi-monthly during growth; dilute liquid fertilizer to half its recommended rate. Propagate by division, seed.

Features: Good choice for borders, containers, massed plantings. Aphid, leaf miner and powdery mildew, rust, wilt disease susceptible.

Name: Coneflower, Purple. *Echinacea purpurea.* ASTERACEAE (COMPOSITAE).

Description: Upright, spreading perennial herb, 2–4 ft. (60–120 cm) tall and wide. Alternate, textured, green, oval to bladelike leaves, 4–8 in. (10–20 cm) long. Tall, pink, purple, red, white, flat or drooping flowers, 3–6 in. (75–150 mm) wide, with dark, conelike centers, in late summer.

Attracts: Birds, butterflies with flowers, pollen, seed.

Plant hardiness: Zones 3–10.

Site/Soil: Full sun–partial shade. Damp–dry, well-drained soil. Fertility: Average. 7.0 pH.

Planting: Space 18–24 in. (45–60 cm) apart after soil warms.

Care: Easy. Allow surface soil to dry between waterings. Fertilize quarterly during growth. Mulch. Propagate by division, seed.

Features: Good choice for backgrounds, borders, windy sites. Japanese beetle, mite and southern blight, downy and powdery mildew, rust susceptible.

Name: Coralbells. *Heuchera sanguinea.* SAXIFRAGACEAE.
Description: Bushy perennial herb, 1–2 ft. (30–60 cm) tall and wide, with tall flower stems above foliage. Hairy, textured, dark green or silver patterned, round to heart-shaped, 5- to 9-lobed, evergreen leaves, to 2 in. (50 mm) long. Many tiny, chartreuse, pink, red, white, bell-like flowers, in clusters, 2–4 in. (50–100 mm) wide, in summer–autumn.
Attracts: Birds, hummingbirds with flowers, nectar, seed.
Plant hardiness: Zones 3–10.
Site/Soil: Full sun–partial shade. Moist, well-drained soil. Fertility: Rich. 6.0–7.0 pH.
Planting: Space 9–15 in. (23–40 cm) apart after frost hazard has passed.
Care: Easy. Keep evenly moist. Fertilize annually in spring. Mulch during winter. Propagate by division, seed.
Features: Good choice for borders, edgings, foregrounds. Mealy bug, nematode, root weevil and stem rot susceptible.

Name: Cornflower; Bachelor's-Button. *Centaurea cyanus.* ASTERACEAE (COMPOSITAE).
Description: Upright, slender annual herb, to 2 ft. (60 cm) tall. Hairy, gray green, narrow, lance-shaped leaves, to 3 in. (75 mm) long, with gray undersides. Many burgundy, blue, pink, red, white, round flowers, to 1½ in. (38 mm) wide, in early summer–autumn. Other *Centaurea* species are prized for their attractive silver foliage. Cultivars include 'Alba', 'Blue Diadem', 'Jubilee Gem', 'Polka Dot'.
Attracts: Birds, butterflies with flowers, insects, seed.
Plant hardiness: Hardy. Self-seeding, zones 3–9.
Site/Soil: Full sun. Moist, well-drained soil. Fertility: Average–low. 6.5–7.0 pH. Tolerates poor soil.
Planting: Space 8–12 in. (20–30 cm) apart after frost hazard has passed. Best sown directly in the garden; avoid transplanting.
Care: Easy. Keep moist. Fertilize monthly during growth. Propagate by seed.
Features: Good choice for beds, borders, edgings, massed plantings. Plant successions at biweekly intervals for continuous blooms. Pest and disease resistant.

Name: Cosmos. *Cosmos bipinnatus, C. sulphureus.* ASTERACEAE (COMPOSITAE).
Description: Upright, branching or bushy annual herbs, 7–10 ft. (2.1–3 m) tall. Shiny, yellow green, featherlike leaves, to 5 in. (13 cm) long. Showy pink, red, violet, yellow flowers, 2–3 in. (50–75 mm) wide, with bright yellow centers, in summer–autumn. Only yellow cosmos, *C. sulphureus*, is yellow flowered.
Attracts: Birds, butterflies with flowers, seed.
Plant hardiness: Tender. Self-seeding, zones 5–11.
Site/Soil: Full–filtered sun. Dry, well-drained, sandy soil. Fertility: Average–low. 7.0–7.5 pH. Blooms best in poor soil.
Planting: Space 1 ft. (30 cm) apart after soil warms. Best sown directly in the garden; avoid transplanting.
Care: Easy. Allow surface soil to dry between waterings. Stake and protect from wind. Avoid fertilizing. Deadhead spent flowers to promote bloom. Propagate by seed.
Features: Good choice for accents, backgrounds, beds, borders. Good for cutting. Pest and disease resistant.

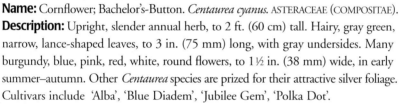

Name: Florist's Geranium. *Pelargonium* species and *P.* × *hortorum*. GERANIACEAE.
Description: About 280 species, many hybrids of mounding annual, perennial herbs and shrubs, to 4 ft. (1.2 m) tall. Textured, mid- to gray green or variegated, rounded, lobed, or ivylike leaves, to 5 in. (13 cm) wide. Many fragrant, mauve, orange, pink, purple, red, white, 5-petaled, star-, saucer-, funnel-, or butterfly-shaped flowers, to 4 in. (10 cm) wide, in clusters, in spring–summer; some are repeat bloomers.
Attracts: Birds, butterflies, hummingbirds with flowers, nectar, pollen.
Plant hardiness: Plant as tender annual, zones 3–7; hardy, zones 8–10.
Site/Soil: Full sun. Moist, well-drained soil. Fertility: Average. 7.0–7.5 pH.
Planting: Space 1 ft. (30 cm) apart after soil warms.
Care: Easy. Allow surface soil to dry between waterings. Deadhead spent flowers to prolong bloom. Cut to ground in autumn after frost, zones 8–10; store containers indoors, zones 3–7. Propagate by division, seed.
Features: Good choice for accents, borders, color, containers, massed plantings. Good for small-space gardens. Mealybug, thrip and mildew, susceptible.

Name: Flossflower; Ageratum. *Ageratum houstonianum.* ASTERACEAE (COMPOSITAE).
Description: Upright annual herb, to 30 in. (75 cm) tall. Hairy, green, heart-shaped, finely toothed leaves, to 5 in. (13 cm) long. Many blue, pink, violet, yellow flowers, in clustered heads, in early summer–autumn. Cultivars include 'Album', 'Blue Blazer', 'North Sea', 'Summer Snow'.
Attracts: Birds, butterflies with flowers, nectar, seed.
Plant hardiness: Tender. Self-seeding, zones 4–11.
Site/Soil: Full sun, zones 2–8; partial shade, zones 9–11. Moist, well-drained soil. Fertility: Rich. 6.5–7.0 pH.
Planting: Space 6–9 in. (15–23 cm) apart. Transplant after frost hazard has passed, zones 2–9; seed for autumn–winter bloom, zones 10–11.
Care: Easy. Keep moist during growth and bloom. Fertilize monthly from planting to bloom. Deadhead spent flowers to prolong bloom. Protect from sun, zones 9–11. Propagate by seed.
Features: Good choice for beds, borders, containers, edgings. Good for cutting. Long-lasting blooms. Scald the stems after picking; soak in cool water before arranging.

Name: Four-O'Clock; Marvel-of-Peru. *Mirabilis jalapa.* NYCTAGINACEAE.
Description: Mounding, shrublike, tuberous perennial herb, to 3 ft. (90 cm) tall. Alternate, green, lance-shaped leaves, 2–5 in. (50–125 mm) long. Many fragrant, pink, red, yellow, white, variegated, flute-shaped, fringed flowers, to 2 in. (50 mm) wide, in summer–autumn, opening in late afternoon.
Attracts: Hummingbirds with flowers, nectar.
Plant hardiness: Plant as tender annual, zones 3–7; hardy, zones 8–11.
Site/Soil: Full sun–partial shade. Damp–dry, well-drained, sandy soil. Fertility: Rich–average. 6.5–7.0 pH. Tolerates poor soil.
Planting: Space 1–2 ft. (30–60 cm) apart after soil warms.
Care: Easy. Keep moist during active growth. Fertilize annually in spring. Lift in autumn and store in dark at 50–60°F (10–16°C), in net bag or open basket of dry peat moss. Propagate by cuttings or by cutting tuber into sections, each with an eye.
Features: Good choice for accents, beds, borders, hedge. Good edging for patios, pools, and water gardens. Pest and disease resistant.

Name: Foxglove. *Digitalis* species. SCROPHULARIACEAE.

Description: About 19 species of upright, slender, biennial or perennial herbs, 2–5 ft. (60–150 cm) tall. Hairy, gray green, oval or lance-shaped, pointed leaves, to 8 in. (20 cm) long, forming a circular, radiating base. Large, showy, mostly yellow, drooping, bell-shaped flowers, 2 in. (50 mm) long, often marked with brown or pink and with brown, purple, white, yellow, sometimes with spotted centers, in summer.

Warning

All parts of foxglove are fatally toxic if ingested. Avoid planting in areas frequented by children and pets.

Attracts: Birds, hummingbirds with flowers, nectar, seed.

Plant hardiness: Zones 2–9.

Site/Soil: Filtered sun–partial shade. Moist, well-drained humus. Fertility: Rich. 6.5–7.0 pH. Supplement with leaf mold.

Planting: Space 15–18 in. (40–45 cm) apart, when soil is workable.

Care: Easy. Keep moist. Fertilize annually in spring. Mulch, zones 2–5. Propagate by division, seed.

Features: Good choice for accents, backgrounds, fences. Leaf spot, Japanese beetle susceptible.

Name: Gladiolus; Sword Lily; Corn Flag. *Gladiolus* species. IRIDACEAE.

Description: About 300 species, many hybrids of upright, narrow, deciduous, perennial corms, 1–6 ft. (30–180 cm) tall. Shiny, green, swordlike, narrow, ribbed leaves, to 32 in. (80 cm) long. Many orange, pink, purple, red, white, yellow, multicolored, striped, upturned, flared, trumpet-shaped, often fragrant flowers, 1–8 in. (25–200 mm) wide, in tiers, in spring zones 7–11; summer, zones 3–6.

Attracts: Hummingbirds with flowers, nectar.

Plant hardiness: Plant as tender annual, zones 3–11; hardy, zones 7–9.

Site/Soil: Full sun. Moist, well-drained, sandy soil. Fertility: Rich–average. 6.5–7.0 pH.

Planting: Space 4–6 in. (10–15 cm) apart, 4–6 in. (10–15 cm) deep, after soil warms.

Care: Easy. Keep moist during growth. Fertilize until flower spikes appear. Mulch. Lift corms in autumn and store in dark at 50–60°F (10–16°C), in net bag or open basket of dry peat moss. Propagate by cormlets, seed.

Features: Good choice for beds, borders, containers, fences. Good for cutting. Deer, rodent and thrip susceptible.

Name: Goldenrod. *Solidago* hybrids. ASTERACEAE (COMPOSITAE).

Description: About 130 species, many hybrids of upright, rhizomatous perennial herbs, to 3 ft. (90 cm) tall. Shiny or hairy, green, lance-shaped, narrow, usually toothed leaves, to 6 in. (15 cm) long. Many tiny, cream, white, yellow flowers in feathery, plumelike clusters, to 10 in. (25 cm) long, in summer–autumn.

Attracts: Birds, butterflies with flowers, pollen, seed.

Plant hardiness: Zones 2–10.

Site/Soil: Full–filtered sun. Damp, well-drained, sandy soil. Fertility: Average–low. 6.5–7.5 pH.

Planting: Space 18–24 in. (45–60 cm) apart after soil warms.

Care: Easy. Allow surface soil to dry between waterings. Fertilize annually in spring. Propagate by division, seed.

Features: Good choice for accents, backgrounds, beds, borders. Invasive, zones 7–10. Mistakenly believed to cause allergic reactions in susceptible individuals. Pest and disease resistant.

Name: Hollyhock. *Alcea rosea (Althaea rosea)*. MALVACEAE.
Description: Upright, narrow biennial herb, to 9 ft. (2.7 m) tall. Textured, green, round leaves, 6–8 in. (15–20 cm) wide, forming a circular, radiating base. Showy maroon, pink, red, white, yellow, saucer-shaped flowers, to 4 in. (10 cm) wide, opening upward along the stalk, in summer–autumn. Dwarf cultivars available.
Attracts: Birds, hummingbirds with flowers, nectar, seed.
Plant hardiness: Zones 2–10.
Site/Soil: Full sun. Moist, well-drained soil. Fertility: Average. 7.0–7.5 pH.
Planting: Space 1 ft. (30 cm) apart. Sow 1-season cultivars when soil is workable; plant 2-season cultivars in early summer to divide and transplant the following spring.
Care: Easy. Keep evenly moist. Stake and protect from wind. Propagate by division, seed.
Features: Good choice for accents, backgrounds, beds. Slug, snail and rust susceptible.

Name: Larkspur. *Delphinium* species. RANUNCULACEAE.
Description: More than 300 species of usually upright, narrow, annual, biennial, and perennial herbs, 1–8 ft. (30–240 cm) tall, 18–36 in. (45–90 cm) wide. Textured, dark green, deep-lobed, fanlike, toothed leaves, to 8 in. (20 cm) wide. Mostly blue or purple, sometimes cream, pink, white, or bicolored, starlike flowers, to 3 in. (8 cm) wide, with black, gold or white centers, in summer. Dwarf cultivars available.
Attracts: Birds, hummingbirds with flowers, nectar, seed.
Plant hardiness: Zones 3–10.
Site/Soil: Full sun–partial shade. Moist, well-drained, humus. Fertility: Rich. 6.5–7.0 pH. Best in low-clay soils.
Planting: Space 18–36 in. (45–90 cm) apart when soil is workable.

> **Warning**
>
> All parts of larkspur are toxic if ingested. Avoid planting in areas frequented by children and pets.

Care: Easy. Keep evenly moist. Fertilize monthly in early and late season. Mulch. Protect from wind. Stake taller cultivars. Deadhead spent blossoms for repeat blooming. Propagate by cuttings, division, seed.
Features: Good choice for backgrounds, beds, edgings. Good for cutting. Slug, snail, aphid and fungal disease susceptible.

Name: Lupine. *Lupinus* species and hybrids. FABACEAE (LEGUMINOSAE).
Description: About 200 species and many hybrids of upright or bushy annual and perennial herbs, 3–5 ft. (90–150 cm) tall. Fuzzy, yellow green, palmlike, deep-lobed leaves, to 4 in. (10 cm) long. Many blue, cream, orange, pink, purple, red, white, yellow, bicolored, pealike flowers, arranged on spikes, to 2 ft. (60 cm) long, in spring–summer.
Attracts: Birds, hummingbirds with flowers, nectar, seed.
Plant hardiness: Most species, zones 3–8; some hardy, zones 2–10.
Site/Soil: Full–filtered sun. Moist–damp, well-drained, sandy soil. Fertility: Rich–low, depending on species. 6.0–7.0 pH.
Planting: Space 2–3 ft. (60–90 cm) apart, after frost hazard has passed.
Care: Easy. Allow surface soil to dry between waterings. Fertilize annually in spring. Protect from wind. Deadhead spent blossoms for autumn bloom. Propagate by division, seed.
Features: Good choice for backgrounds, beds, borders, fences. Disease resistant. Lupine aphid susceptible.

Name: Marigold. *Tagetes erecta.* ASTERACEAE (COMPOSITAE).

Description: Many cultivars of mounding, bushy, annual herbs, to 3 ft. (90 cm) tall. Fragrant, smooth, deep green, feather-shaped, deeply lobed, toothed leaves, to 3 in. (75 mm) long. Many, cream, gold, white, yellow, round, wavy-fringed flowers, to 2½ in. (65 mm) wide, in summer–autumn. Many varied and dwarf cultivars available.

Attracts: Birds, butterflies with flowers, pollen.

Plant hardiness: Semi-hardy. Zones 3–10.

Site/Soil: Full sun. Moist, well-drained soil. Fertility: Average. 6.5–7.0 pH.

Planting: Space 8–16 in. (20–40 cm) apart. Start seed indoors 6–8 weeks before the last frost; sow seeds outdoors 2–3 weeks after the last frost.

Care: Easy. Keep evenly moist. Fertilize monthly during growth. Deadhead spent flowers to prolong bloom. Propagate by seed.

Features: Good choice for beds, borders, containers, edgings. Aphid, leaf hopper and powdery mildew susceptible.

Name: Michaelmas Daisy. *Aster novi-belgii.* ASTERACEAE (COMPOSITAE).

Description: Upright, bushy, rhizomatous perennial, to 4 ft. (1.2 m) tall and wide, with tall flower stalks. Hairy, deep green, lance-shaped leaves, 3–5 in. (75–125 mm) long. Showy blue, pink, purple, red, white, daisylike flowers, to 2½ in. (65 mm) wide, in late summer–autumn.

Attracts: Birds, butterflies with flowers, pollen, seed.

Plant hardiness: Zones 2–9.

Site/Soil: Full–filtered sun. Moist, well-drained, sandy soil. Fertility: Rich–average. 6.0–7.0 pH.

Planting: Space 3–4 ft. (90–120 cm) apart when soil is workable.

Care: Easy. Keep evenly moist. Fertilize monthly during growth. Deadhead spent flowers to promote bloom. Divide when crowded. Propagate by cuttings, division.

Features: Good choice for accents, backgrounds, containers, massed plantings and water feature margins. Good for cutting. Very invasive. Pest and disease resistant.

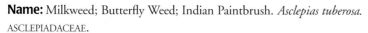

Name: Milkweed; Butterfly Weed; Indian Paintbrush. *Asclepias tuberosa.* ASCLEPIADACEAE.

Description: Upright and branching, hairy perennial herb, 2–3 ft. (60–90 cm) tall, 12–18 in. (30–45 cm) wide. Smooth, green, lance-shaped leaves, to 4½ in. (11 cm) long, in spirals or clusters. Many showy, orange, red, yellow, starlike flowers, to ⅓ in. (9 mm) wide, with light-colored centers, in broad, flat, mounding clusters, in summer.

Attracts: Birds, butterflies, hummingbirds with flowers, nectar, pollen, seed.

Plant hardiness: Zones 3–9.

Site/Soil: Full sun. Dry, well-drained soil. Fertility: Low. 6.5–7.0 pH.

Planting: Space 12–18 in. (30–45 cm) apart. Plant in early spring after frost hazard has passed, zones 3–6; autumn, zones 7–9.

Care: Easy. Water when soil is thoroughly dry. Drought tolerant. Avoid fertilizing. Propagate by division, seed.

Features: Good choice for accents, beds, borders, containers. Good for cutting. Somewhat invasive. Pest and disease resistant.

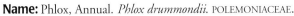

Name: Nasturtium, Garden. *Tropaeolum majus.* TROPAEOLACEAE.
Description: Climbing, mounding, or trailing, succulent annual herb, to 3 ft. (90 cm) tall and wide. Shiny, deep green, round, parasol-shaped leaves, to 3 in. (75 mm) wide. Many fragrant, orange, pink, red, white, yellow, multicolored, deep-throated flowers, to 2½ in. (65 mm) wide, in summer–autumn. Double-flowered and dwarf cultivars available.
Attracts: Birds, butterflies, hummingbirds with flowers, nectar, seed.
Plant hardiness: Tender. Self-seeding, zones 6–10.
Site/Soil: Full–filtered sun. Moist, well-drained, sandy soil. Fertility: Rich–low. 6.5–7.0 pH.
Planting: Space 8–12 in. (20–30 cm) apart after soil warms.
Care: Easy. Keep evenly moist. Avoid fertilizing. Deadhead spent flowers to prolong bloom. Propagate by seed.
Features: Good choice for hanging baskets, borders, containers, edgings. Edible flowers. Somewhat invasive. Aphid, leaf miner and fusarium wilt susceptible.

Name: Phlox, Annual. *Phlox drummondii.* POLEMONIACEAE.
Description: Many cultivars of mounding annual herbs, to 20 in. (50 cm) tall, with hairy stems. Alternating pairs of green, lance-shaped, narrow or oval, pointed leaves, to 2 in. (50 mm) long. Many cream, pink, purple, red, white, starlike flowers, to 1 in. (25 mm) wide, in tightly grouped clusters, in summer–autumn.
Attracts: Butterflies, hummingbirds with flowers, nectar, seed.
Plant hardiness: Semi-hardy. Zones 3–10.
Site/Soil: Full sun–partial shade. Moist–dry, well-drained soil. Fertility: Rich–average. 6.5–7.0 pH.
Planting: Space 10–12 in. (25–30 cm) apart. Start indoors, transplant after frost hazard has passed, zones 3–6; sow outdoors when soil warms, zones 7–10.
Care: Easy. Keep evenly moist. Fertilize monthly. Pinch or shear growth tips to promote bushiness, prolong bloom. Propagate by seed.
Features: Good choice for beds, borders, containers, edgings, ground cover. Powdery mildew susceptible.

Name: Pink. *Dianthus* species. CARYOPHYLLACEAE.
Description: About 300 species, many cultivars of compact, annual, biennial, or perennial herbs, to 1 ft. (30 cm) tall, 12–15 in. (30–38 cm) wide. Shiny, mostly gray green, narrow, grasslike evergreen leaves, to 2 in. (50 mm) long. Fragrant, showy, pink, rose, white, occasionally yellow, bicolor, lacy flowers, 1–1½ in. (25–38 mm) wide, in spring–summer.
Attracts: Birds, butterflies, hummingbirds with flowers, nectar, seed.
Plant hardiness: Zones 4–10.
Site/Soil: Full sun. Damp, well-drained, sandy soil. Fertility: Rich. 7.0–8.0 pH.
Planting: Space 12–15 in. (30–38 cm) apart. Plant after frost hazard has passed, zones 4–7; late summer or autumn, zones 8–10.
Care: Easy. Allow surface soil to dry between waterings. Mulch lightly to protect from cold, zones 4–6. Propagate by cuttings, division, layering, seed.
Features: Good choice for accents, borders, containers, walls. Good for cutting. Rust, fusarium wilt susceptible.

Name: Sage. *Salvia* species, hybrids, and cultivars. LAMIACEAE (LABIATAE).
Description: Over 900 species and many cultivars of annual, biennial, or perennial herbs and shrubs, with widely varied habits, usually fragrant foliage, and most flower colors. Cultivated species include creeping, desert, Dolomite, garden, gentian, golden, hummingbird (*S. spathacea*), mealycup, Mexican, purple, roseleaf, silver, and tropical sage. Blooms spring–autumn, depending on species.
Attracts: Bees, birds, butterflies, hummingbirds with flowers, nectar.
Plant hardiness: Zones 4–10.
Site/Soil: Full sun. Dry, well-drained humus. Fertility: Average–low. 6.0–7.5 pH.
Planting: Space 10–24 in. (25–60 cm) apart when soil is workable.
Care: Easy. Keep moist until established; drought tolerant thereafter. Mulch, zones 4–6. Propagate by cuttings, division, seed.
Features: Good choice for borders, edgings, mixed plantings. Scale, whitefly and leaf spot, rust susceptible.

Name: Snapdragon; Garden Snapdragon. *Antirrhinum majus.* SCROPHULARIACEAE.
Description: Upright, climbing, vining perennial herb, to 3 ft. (90 cm) tall. Shiny, medium green, lance-shaped leaves, to 3 in. (75 mm) long. Many orange, pink, red, white, yellow, bicolored, 2-lipped flowers, to 2 in. (50 mm) long, in spring–early summer. Dwarf cultivars available.
Attracts: Birds, butterflies, hummingbirds with flowers, nectar, pollen.
Plant hardiness: Hardy. Plant as annual, zones 3–7; hardy, zones 8–11.
Site/Soil: Full–filtered sun. Moist, well-drained humus. Fertility: Rich. 7.0 pH.
Planting: Space 4–6 in. (10–15 cm) apart, when soil is workable.
Care: Easy. Keep moist; avoid overhead watering of foliage to prevent rust. Pinch stem tips when plant reaches 2–4 in. (50–100 mm) tall to promote bushiness and flowering. Propagate by seed.
Features: Good choice for beds, edgings, fences, trellises. Good for cutting. Aphid, leaf miner, whitefly and rust susceptible.

Name: Statice; Sea Lavender. *Limonium platyphyllum (L. latifolium).* PLUMBAGINACEAE.
Description: Bushy, spreading, shrublike, woody perennial herb, to 30 in. (75 cm) tall, 3 ft. (90 cm) wide. Hairy, textured, deep green, sword-shaped, oblong to elliptical leaves, to 10 in. (25 cm) long. Tiny, blue, lavender, white, lacy flowers with blue violet centers, in cloudlike, pyramidal, loosely branched, upright clusters, to 6 in. (15 cm) wide, in spring–summer.
Attracts: Birds, butterflies with flowers, pollen.
Plant hardiness: Plant as annual, zones 3–4. Self-seeding, zones 5–10.
Site/Soil: Full sun. Moist, well-drained, sandy soil. Fertility: Average–low. Salt tolerant. 6.0–8.0 pH.
Planting: Space 18 in. (45 cm) apart after soil warms.
Care: Moderate–challenging. Keep evenly moist until established; drought tolerant thereafter. Fertilize annually in spring. Stake, protect from wind. Propagate by division, seed.
Features: Good choice for accents, beds, borders, edgings, and water-feature margins. Good for cutting, drying. Pest and disease resistant.

Name: Sunflower. *Helianthus* species. ASTERACEAE (COMPOSITAE).
Description: About 150 species of upright, narrow or bushy annual and perennial herbs, 3–7 ft. (90–215 cm) tall, 18–24 in. (45–60 cm) wide. Alternate or opposite, coarse-textured, yellow green, usually coarsely toothed leaves. Single or double, yellow, round flowers, 3–12 in. (75–300 mm) wide, with dark centers, as single or clustersed blossoms, in summer–autumn.
Attracts: Birds, butterflies with flowers, insects, pollen, seed.
Plant hardiness: Zones 4–8.
Site/Soil: Full sun–partial shade. Moist, well-drained soil. Fertility: Average. 5.0–7.0 pH.
Planting: Space 18–36 in. (45–90 cm) apart after soil warms.
Care: Easy. Keep moist. Fertilize semi-monthly. Stake tallest cultivars. Propagate by division, seed.
Features: Good choice for borders, massed plantings. Good for cutting. Stalk borer, sunflower maggot, sunflower moth larvae and powdery mildew, rust susceptible.

Name: Thistle, Globe. *Echinops* species. ASTERACEAE (COMPOSITAE).
Description: About 100 species of upright, spreading, biennial and perennial herbs, 3–4 ft. (90–120 cm) tall, 18–24 in. (45–60 cm) wide. Spiny, hairy, deep green, thistlelike, toothed, coarse-textured leaves, to 1 ft. (30 cm) long, usually with white undersides. Spiny blue, white, globe-shaped flowers, in dense armored clusters, 2–3 in. (50–75 mm) wide, in summer–autumn.
Attracts: Birds, butterflies with flowers, seed.
Plant hardiness: Zones 4–8.
Site/Soil: Full sun–partial shade. Damp, well-drained, sandy soil. Fertility: Rich–average. 5.0–6.0 pH.
Planting: Space 18–24 in. (45–60 cm) apart when soil is workable.
Care: Easy–moderate. Allow surface soil to dry between waterings. Stake in rich soil. Thin regularly. Propagate by cuttings, division, seed.
Features: Good choice for accents, backgrounds. Good for cutting, drying. Pest and disease resistant.

Name: Tickseed; Coreopsis. *Coreopsis* species. ASTERACEAE (COMPOSITAE).
Description: Over 100 species of upright, narrow, annual or perennial herbs, 6–36 in. (15–90 cm) tall, 1 ft. (30 cm) wide. Shiny, deep green, long, straplike, toothed or lobed leaves, to 3 in. (75 mm) long. Many brownish orange or yellow, rose, bicolor, daisylike flowers, 3 in. (75 mm) wide, with contrasting centers, in summer–autumn.
Attracts: Birds, butterflies with flowers, pollen, seed.
Plant hardiness: Zones 4–10.
Site/Soil: Full sun. Damp, well-drained soil. Fertility: Rich–low. 5.0–6.0 pH.
Planting: Space 12–18 in. (30–45 cm) apart after soil warms, zones 4–8; autumn, zones 9–10.
Care: Very easy. Allow surface soil to dry between waterings. Fertilize annually in spring. Deadhead spent flowers. Propagate from cuttings, division, seed.
Features: Good choice for borders, edgings, foregrounds. Good for cutting. Chewing insects and leaf spot, powdery mildew, rust susceptible.

Name: Verbena. *Verbena* species. VERBENACEAE.

Description: About 200 species of upright or low and spreading annual and perennial herbs or shrubs, 8–18 in. (20–45 cm) tall. Opposite, hairy, deep green, oval, bluntly toothed leaves, to 4 in. (10 cm) long. Many pink, purple, red, white, yellow, broad, flat flowers, ½ in. (12 mm) wide, in clusters on wiry stems, in spring–autumn.

Attracts: Birds, butterflies, hummingbirds with flowers, nectar, seed.

Plant hardiness: Plant as annual, zones 3–7; hardy, zones 8–9.

Site/Soil: Full sun. Moist, well-drained soil. Fertility: Rich–average. 6.5–7.0 pH.

Planting: Space 1–2 ft. (30–60 cm) apart, depending on variety, when frost hazard has passed.

Care: Easy. Keep moist; avoid overhead watering of foliage to prevent fungal disease. Propagate by cuttings, division.

Features: Good choice for borders, containers, edgings. Invasive, zones 8–9. Budworm, verbena leaf miner, verbena yellow woolly-bear caterpillar and powdery mildew susceptible.

Name: Yarrow. *Achillea* species. ASTERACEAE (COMPOSITAE).

Description: Almost 100 species of erect, open, fragrant, semi-deciduous perennial herbs, 6–54 in. (15–135 cm) tall, 12–18 in. (30–45 cm) wide. Fragrant, soft-textured, gray green, green, silver, finely cut, often toothed leaves, to 8 in. (20 cm) long. Many pink, red, white, yellow flowers, in flat-topped clusters, 3–5 in. (75–125 mm) wide, in spring or continually blooming, depending on species. Evergreen, zones 9–10.

Attracts: Birds, butterflies with flowers, insects, pollen, scent.

Plant hardiness: Zones 3–10.

Site/Soil: Full sun. Dry, well-drained soil. Fertility: Average–low. 7.0 pH.

Planting: Space 1–2 ft. (30–60 cm) apart. Plant in spring, zones 3–8; autumn, zones 9–10.

Care: Easy. Keep moist until established; drought tolerant thereafter. Fertilize annually in spring. Stake tall cultivars. Propagate by division.

Features: Good choice for accents, beds, borders, massed plantings. Good for cutting, drying. Pest resistant. Powdery mildew, stem rot susceptible.

Name: Zinnia. *Zinnia elegans* and hybrids. ASTERACEAE (COMPOSITAE).

Description: Many cultivars, hybrids of bushy annual herbs, 1–4 ft. (30–120 cm) tall. Opposite, softly textured, green, lance-shaped or oval, pointed leaves, to 5 in. (13 cm) long. Many round, green, orange, pink, purple, red, yellow, either double, quilled, or crested flowers, 1–7 in. (25–175 mm) wide, in summer–autumn.

Attracts: Birds, butterflies, hummingbirds with flowers, pollen, seed.

Plant hardiness: Tender. Self-seeding, zones 4–11.

Site/Soil: Full sun. Moist, well-drained soil. Fertility: Rich–average. 7.0–7.5 pH.

Planting: Space 6–12 in. (15–30 cm) apart after soil warms.

Care: Easy. Keep moist; avoid overhead watering of flower buds to prevent fungal disease. Fertilize quarterly. Deadhead spent flowers. Propagate by seed.

Features: Good choice for beds, borders, edgings. Good for cutting. Japanese beetle, borer and powdery mildew susceptible.

SHRUBS AND SMALL TREES

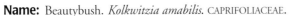

Name: Barberry. *Berberis* species. BERBERIDACEAE.

Description: About 500 species of medium-growth, spiny, dense, deciduous or evergreen shrubs, 4–8 ft. (1.2–2.5 m) tall, depending on species. Shiny, hollylike, green, red, yellow, or variegated leaves, 1–3 in. (25–75 mm) long, turning red, purple in autumn. Many, cup-shaped, yellow to red flowers in spring, forming hanging branched clusters, to 4 in. (10 cm) long, with blue, red, yellow berries in autumn.

Attracts: Birds, hummingbirds with flowers, berries.

Plant hardiness: Zones 3–9, depending on species.

Site/Soil: Full–partial sun. Dry–moist, well-drained soil. Fertility: Average–low. 5.0–8.0 pH.

Planting: Space 2–6 ft. (60–180 cm) apart, depending on species and use.

Care: Easy. Allow surface soil to dry between waterings until established. Fertilize annually in spring. Prune by removing oldest wood. Protect from sun, wind. Propagate by cuttings, layering, seed.

Features: Good choice for accents, barriers, hedges. Drought, humidity, smog tolerant. Some species regulated to prevent stem rust disease.

Name: Beautybush. *Kolkwitzia amabilis.* CAPRIFOLIACEAE.

Description: Fast-growing, arching, deciduous, herbaceous shrub, to 15 ft. (4.5 m) tall and wide, with brown, flaking bark. Textured, gray green, oval leaves, to 3 in. (75 mm) long, sometimes turning red in autumn. Showy pink, 5-petaled flowers with bristly, yellow centers, to ½ in. (12 mm) long, in late spring, forming dense clusters, with distinctive, bristly, brown fruit in summer.

Attracts: Birds, hummingbirds with flowers, fruit.

Plant hardiness: Plant as annual, zones 4–5; hardy, zones 6–8.

Site/Soil: Full sun. Moist, well-drained soil. Fertility: Rich–low. 6.0–8.0 pH.

Planting: Space 12 ft. (3.7 m) apart.

Care: Easy. Keep moist. Fertilize monthly spring–summer. Mulch, zones 4–5. Prune after bloom. Protect from sun in hot climates. Propagate by cuttings.

Features: Good choice for backgrounds, borders, fences. Pest and disease resistant.

Name: Butterfly Bush. *Buddleia davidii.* BUDDLEIACEAE.

Description: Several cultivars of wide, willowlike, mostly deciduous shrubs, 4–15 ft. (1.2–4.5 m) tall. Feltlike or hairy, gray green to dark green, narrow, pointed leaves, 3–5 in. (75–125 mm) long. Small, fragrant, lilaclike, orange, pink, purple, white, or yellow flowers in spring–summer form arching spikes to 10 in. (25 cm) long, with dry, berrylike seedpods in autumn.

Attracts: Birds, butterflies, hummingbirds with flowers, insects, seed.

Plant hardiness: Plant as annual, zones 5–6; hardy, zones 7–10.

Site/Soil: Full–partial sun. Dry–moist, well-drained soil. Fertility: Average–low. 7.0 pH.

Planting: Space 3 ft. (90 cm) apart.

Care: Easy. Allow surface soil to dry between waterings. Fertilize monthly. Deadhead. Prune in spring: to ground in cold-winter climates; one-third to ground in mild-winter climates. Propagate by cuttings, seed.

Features: Good choice for backgrounds, borders, containers. Pest and disease resistant.

Name: Cotoneaster, Spreading. *Cotoneaster divaricatus.* ROSACEAE.

Description: Slow-growing deciduous shrub, to 6 ft. (1.8 m) tall and 10 ft. (3 m) wide. Branches bear thorny spurs. Shiny, dark green, smooth, oval, pointed leaves, to ¾ in. (19 mm) long. Pink or red flowers, to ½ in. (12 mm) wide, in spring, form red berries in autumn, ½ in. (12 mm) wide.

Attracts: Birds, hummingbirds with berries, flowers, insects.

Plant hardiness: Plant as annual, zones 5–6; hardy, zones 7–9.

Site/Soil: Partial shade. Moist, well-drained soil. Fertility: Average–low. 6.5–7.0 pH.

Planting: Space 5 ft. (1.5 m) apart.

Care: Easy. Allow surface soil to dry between waterings until established. Fertilize monthly spring–autumn. Minimal pruning. Protect from frost, zones 5–6. Propagate by cuttings, seed.

Features: Good choice for barriers, ground cover, hedges, paths. Drought, salt, wind tolerant. Pest and disease resistant.

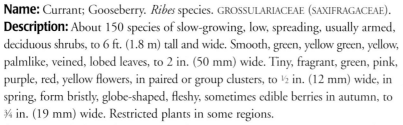

Name: Currant; Gooseberry. *Ribes* species. GROSSULARIACEAE (SAXIFRAGACEAE).

Description: About 150 species of slow-growing, low, spreading, usually armed, deciduous shrubs, to 6 ft. (1.8 m) tall and wide. Smooth, green, yellow green, yellow, palmlike, veined, lobed leaves, to 2 in. (50 mm) wide. Tiny, fragrant, green, pink, purple, red, yellow flowers, in paired or group clusters, to ½ in. (12 mm) wide, in spring, form bristly, globe-shaped, fleshy, sometimes edible berries in autumn, to ¾ in. (19 mm) wide. Restricted plants in some regions.

Attracts: Birds, butterflies, hummingbirds with flowers, fruit.

Plant hardiness: Zones 3–10, depending on species.

Site/Soil: Full sun–partial shade. Moist–dry, well-drained soil, depending on species. Fertility: Rich–average. 6.0–7.0 pH.

Planting: Space 4–5 ft. (1.2–1.5 m) apart.

Care: Easy. Keep moist until established; some species drought tolerant thereafter. Fertilize annually in spring. Propagate by cuttings, layering, seed.

Features: Good choice for backgrounds, fences. Black stem wheat rust susceptible and white pine blister rust host plant.

Name: Elder; Elderberry. *Sambucus* species. CAPRIFOLIACEAE.

Description: About 20 species of fast-growing, open, deciduous shrubs or small trees, 6–30 ft. (1.8–9 m) tall. Opposite, shiny, bronze, green, purple, featherlike, 5- to 7-lobed, toothed leaves, to 1 ft. (30 cm) long. Tiny, cream, pink, white flowers, in flat clusters, to 10 in. (25 cm) wide, in spring, form purple, red, round, sometimes fleshy, edible berries in autumn.

Attracts: Birds with fruit.

Plant hardiness: Zones 2–10, depending on species.

Site/Soil: Full–filtered sun. Moist, well-drained soil. Fertility: Rich–average. 6.0–7.5 pH.

Planting: Space 10–12 ft. (3–3.7 m) apart.

Care: Easy. Keep moist until established; drought tolerant thereafter. Fertilize annually in spring. Prune to promote bushiness. Propagate by seed, suckers.

Features: Good choice for accents, backgrounds. Good for pies, preserves. Pest resistant. Powdery mildew susceptible.

Name: Firethorn. *Pyracantha* species. ROSACEAE.

Description: About 6 species of medium-growing, upright or spreading, dense, semi-evergreen, thorny shrubs, 6–20 ft. (1.8–6.0 m) tall, depending on species. Shiny or leathery, green, lance-shaped leaves, ¾–4 in. (19–100 mm) long. Many small white flowers in spring, in dense, mounding clusters, form bright red berries in autumn, persisting to winter.

Attracts: Bees, birds with flowers, berries.

Plant hardiness: Zones 4–9, depending on species. All species ground hardy, zones 7–9.

Site/Soil: Full sun. Moist, well-drained. Fertility: Average. 6.0–8.0 pH.

Planting: Space 6–8 ft. (1.8–2.4 m) apart.

Care: Moderate. Allow surface soil to dry between waterings until established. Fertilize annually in spring. Prune after bloom, using care to avoid sharp thorns. Propagate by cuttings, grafting, layering, seed.

Features: Good choice for accents, barriers, ground cover. Best in dry climates. Avoid transplanting. Apple scab, fireblight susceptible.

Name: Fuchsia, Hybrid. *Fuchsia* × *hybrida*. ONAGRACEAE.

Description: Many hybrids of slow-growing, semi-evergreen or evergreen shrubs, to 12 ft. (3.7 m) tall. Shiny, bronze, green, purple, oval to lance-shaped, finely toothed leaves, to 2 in. (50 mm) long. Showy, blue, bronze, pink, purple, red, violet, nodding, cup-shaped flowers, to 3 in. (75 mm) long, with long pink, red, white sepals in summer, form purple, seedy berries in autumn.

Attracts: Birds, hummingbirds with flowers, nectar, pollen, berries.

Plant hardiness: Tender. Zones 7–10.

Site/Soil: Full–filtered sun, zones 7–8; shade, zones 9–10. Moist, well-drained humus. Fertility: Rich. 6.0–7.0 pH.

Planting: Space 3–4 ft. (90–120 cm) apart.

Care: Moderate. Keep evenly moist. Fertilize monthly during active growth. Deadhead spent flowers to prolong bloom. Prune sparingly. Protect from frost, zones 7–8; sun, zones 9–10.

Features: Good choice for borders, containers. Aphid and chlorosis susceptible.

Name: Holly. *Ilex* species. AQUIFOLIACEAE.

Description: Nearly 400 species of medium- to slow-growing, rounded, dense, mostly evergreen shrubs or small trees, 10–50 ft. (3–15 m) tall depending on species. Shiny, leathery, deep green, toothed, usually spiny leaves, to 4 in. (10 cm) long. Inconspicuous white or green flowers form round, black or red berries on female trees, in clusters, to 6 in. (15 cm) long, in autumn. Plant a pollinating male tree with one or more female trees.

Attracts: Birds with berries.

Plant hardiness: Zones 4–8, depending on species. Ground hardy, zones 7–8.

Site/Soil: Full sun. Moist, well-drained soil. Fertility: Average. 6.0–7.0 pH.

Planting: Space 8–12 ft. (2.4–3.7 m) apart, depending on species.

Care: Moderate. Keep moist. Fertilize annually in spring. Mulch. Prune in spring. Protect from sun, wind in hot climates. Propagate by cuttings, grafting, seed.

Features: Good choice for accents, borders, backgrounds, hedges in cottage, formal, small-space gardens. Mealybug, leaf miner, scale susceptible.

Name: Jessamine, Night; Night Jasmine. *Cestrum nocturnum.* SOLANACEAE.

Description: Bushy, climbing or spreading, semi-evergreen tropical shrub, to 12 ft. (3.7 m) tall. Shiny, deep green, oval, slender leaves, 4–7 in. (10–18 cm) long. Many very fragrant, cream, white, green-tinged, flute-shaped flowers, to 1 in. (25 mm) long, in summer, opening in evening, form white berries in autumn.

Attracts: Birds, hummingbirds with flowers, berries.

Plant hardiness: Tender. Zones 8–11.

Site/Soil: Full sun. Moist, well-drained humus. Fertility: Rich. 6.0–7.0 pH.

Planting: Space 8–10 ft. (2.4–3 m) apart.

Care: Moderate. Allow surface soil to dry between waterings. Fertilize monthly during active growth. Prune after bloom. Protect from frost, zones 8–9. Propagate by cuttings, seed.

Features: Good choice for backgrounds, containers, fences, trellises. Pest and disease resistant.

Name: Lavender. *Lavandula* species. LAMIACEAE (LABIATAE).

Description: About 20 species of fast-growing, upright, dense, semi-evergreen perennial herbs and shrubs, 1–4 ft. (30–120 cm) tall. Many tiny, fragrant, blue, pink, purple flowers, in dense, plumelike clusters, to 10 in. (25 cm) long, in summer. Woolly, gray to gray green, needlelike leaves, to 2 in. (50 mm) long.

Attracts: Birds, butterflies, hummingbirds with flowers, seed.

Plant hardiness: Zones 7–10.

Site/Soil: Full sun. Dry, well-drained soil. Fertility: Average–low. 6.5–7.5 pH.

Planting: Space 12–18 in. (30–45 cm) apart after frost hazard has passed.

Care: Easy. Allow surface soil to dry between waterings. Avoid fertilizing. Mulch in winter, zones 7–8. Prune after bloom. Propagate by cuttings, division.

Features: Good choice for accents, borders, containers, hedges. Good for cutting, drying. Pest and disease resistant.

Name: Lilac. *Syringa* species. OLEACEAE.

Description: Over 30 species of fast-growing, spreading, dense, deciduous shrubs, 5–20 ft. (1.5–6.0 m) tall. Shiny, dark green, smooth, oval leaves, to 5 in. (13 cm) long. Tiny, fragrant, lavender, pink, purple, white flowers in spring forming large showy clusters, 3½–10 in. (90–250 mm) long, with leathery seed-filled capsules in summer. First blooms 2–3 years after planting. Most require chilling to bloom.

Attracts: Birds, butterflies with flowers, nectar, seed.

Plant hardiness: Zones 3–9.

Site/Soil: Full sun–partial shade. Moist, well-drained soil. Fertility: Rich. 7.0–7.5 pH.

Planting: Space 5–10 ft. (1.5–3 m) apart. Transplants readily.

Care: Moderate. Keep evenly moist. Fertilize quarterly, spring–autumn. Deadhead spent flowers to prolong bloom. Prune sparingly after bloom. Propagate by cuttings, layering.

Features: Good choice for accents, beds, borders, edgings, fences. Invasive. Deer-resistant. Powdery mildew susceptible.

Name: Mahonia; Oregon Grape. *Mahonia* species. BERBERIDACEAE.

Description: Over 100 species of slow-growing, spreading, broad-leaved, evergreen shrubs, to 12 ft. (3.7 m) tall, depending on species. Shiny, blue green, leathery, toothed, usually spiny leaves, to 3 in. (75 mm) long, arranged along the stem in groups of 5 or 7, and tinged red in autumn. Tiny, fragrant, yellow, bell-shaped flowers in spring, to ½ in. (12 mm) wide, in narrow spiking clusters, form black or blue, blueberry-like, mealy fruit in autumn.

Attracts: Birds, butterflies, hummingbirds with flowers, nectar, pollen, fruit.

Plant hardiness: Zones 4–8, depending on species.

Site/Soil: Partial–full shade. Moist, well-drained humus. Fertility: Rich. 5.5–6.5 pH.

Planting: Space 5–7 ft. (1.5–2.1 m) apart.

Care: Easy–moderate. Keep evenly moist. Fertilize quarterly spring–autumn. Mulch, zones 7–8. Avoid pruning. Propagate by cuttings, layering, seed.

Features: Good choice for accents, backgrounds, barriers, fences, hedges. *M. aquifolium* is drought tolerant. Pest and disease resistant.

Name: Rosemary. *Rosmarinus officinalis.* LAMIACEAE (LABIATAE).

Description: Fast-growing, upright and spreading or trailing, evergreen shrub, to 4 ft. (1.2 m) tall and wide. Fragrant, shiny, deep or olive green, leathery, needlelike leaves, to 1½ in. (38 mm) long. Many tiny, light blue, violet flowers, in spiking clusters, to 4 in. (10 cm) long, in summer–autumn.

Attracts: Birds, butterflies, hummingbirds with flowers, pollen.

Plant hardiness: Plant as annual, zones 5–6; hardy, zones 7–11.

Site/Soil: Full sun. Damp–dry, well-drained soil. Fertility: Low. 7.0–8.0 pH. Salt, poor soil tolerant.

Planting: Space 2–3 ft. (60–90 cm) apart.

Care: Easy. Allow surface soil to dry between waterings. Avoid fertilizing. Prune to shape growth. Propagate by cuttings, seed.

Features: Good choice for hanging baskets, containers, ground cover. Pest and disease resistant.

Name: Serviceberry; Juneberry; Shadbush. *Amelanchier* species. ROSACEAE.

Description: About 25 species of medium-growing, upright, round-crowned, open, deciduous shrubby trees, to 40 ft. (12 m) tall, depending on species, often with multiple trunks, and with silver gray, white bark. Shiny, deep green, oval, pointed, toothed leaves, to 3 in. (75 mm) long, turning orange, yellow in autumn. Many ribbonlike, white flowers, to 2 in. (50 mm) long, in clusters in spring as leaves emerge, form edible, deep blue, berrylike fruit, to ⅓ in. (8 mm) wide, in summer.

Attracts: Bees, birds with flowers, fruit.

Plant hardiness: Zones 1–8, depending on species.

Site/Soil: Full sun. Moist, well-drained soil. Fertility: Average-low. 6.0–7.0 pH. Best with winter chill.

Planting: Space 8–15 ft. (2.5–4.5 m) apart.

Care: Moderate. Keep evenly moist. Fertilize annually in spring until established. Prune in autumn; remove suckers to maintain treelike appearance. Propagate by seed, suckers.

Features: Good choice for accents, borders, containers, margins, paths, screens. Drops flowers, fruit, requiring maintenance. Lacewing, scale, spider mite and fireblight susceptible.

Name: Snowberry; Coralberry. *Symphoricarpos* species. CAPRIFOLIACEAE.

Description: About 16 species of fast-growing, upright or spreading, deciduous shrubs, 2–6 ft. (60–180 cm) tall, depending on species. Matte, green, round or oval, slightly lobed leaves, to 2 in. (50 mm) long. Many tiny green, pink, white flowers, in grapelike clusters, in spring–summer, form white, round, mealy, seed-filled fruit, to ¼ in. (6 mm) wide, in autumn.

Attracts: Birds, butterflies, hummingbirds with flowers, pollen, fruit.

Plant hardiness: Zones 3–9, depending on species.

Site/Soil: Filtered sun. Damp, well-drained soil. Fertility: Average. 6.5–7.5 pH.

Planting: Space 1–3 ft. (30–90 cm) apart, depending on species.

Care: Easy. Allow soil surface to dry between waterings. Fertilize annually in spring. Prune to shape, control growth. Propagate by cuttings, division, seed.

Features: Good choice for backgrounds, ground cover, slopes. Aphid, caterpillar, scale and anthracnose susceptible.

Name: Verbena, Shrub; Lantana. *Lantana* hybrids. VERBENACEAE.

Description: Many hybrids of fast-growing, evergreen, often thorny, tropical shrubs, to 6 ft. (1.8 m) tall and wide. Fragrant, shiny, deep green, oval, pointed leaves, to 5 in. (13 cm) long. Many tiny, cream, gold, orange, pink, purple, red, yellow, bicolored flowers, in flat, mounded, or spiking clusters, to 3 in. (75 mm) wide, in summer or continually blooming. Many hybrid cultivars available with spreading or tall habits.

Attracts: Butterflies, hummingbirds with flowers, nectar.

Plant hardiness: Plant as tender annual, zones 6–8; hardy, zones 9–10.

Site/Soil: Full sun. Damp, well-drained sandy soil. Fertility: Rich–average. 6.5–7.5 pH.

Planting: Space 3–4 ft. (90–120 cm) apart.

Care: Easy. Allow surface soil to dry between waterings. Fertilize annually in spring. Prune to promote bushiness. Propagate by cuttings, seed.

Features: Good choice for hanging baskets, borders, containers, ground cover. Mealybug and orthezia susceptible.

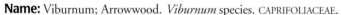

Name: Viburnum; Arrowwood. *Viburnum* species. CAPRIFOLIACEAE.

Description: More than 225 species of fast-growing, upright, dense, deciduous or semi-evergreen shrubs and small trees, 6–12 ft. (1.8–3.7 m) tall, depending on species. Hairy, deep green, purple-tinged, round or oval, coarsely toothed leaves, 4–5 in. (10–13 cm) long, turning orange, red in autumn. Many tiny, white, cup-shaped flowers, in dense mounding clusters, to 8 in. (20 cm) wide, in summer, form red, berrylike, seed-filled fruit in autumn.

Attracts: Birds, butterflies with flowers, pollen, seed.

Plant hardiness: Zones 5–8.

Site/Soil: Filtered sun–partial shade. Moist, well-drained soil. Fertility: Rich. 6.5–7.0 pH.

Planting: Space 5–10 ft. (1.5–3 m) apart, depending on species.

Care: Easy. Keep evenly moist. Fertilize monthly, spring–autumn. Prune to promote bushiness, shear to shape. Propagate by cuttings, grafting, layering, seed.

Features: Good choice for backgrounds, borders, mixed plantings. Aphid, scale, spider mite, thrip and powdery mildew susceptible.

VINES

Name: Cape Honeysuckle. *Tecoma capensis (Tecomaria capensis).* BIGNONIACEAE.
Description: Fast-growing, semi-evergreen, tropical shrub, to 8 ft. (2.4 m) tall and wide, or climbing vine, to 30 ft. (9 m) long. Shiny, deep green, palmlike, 5- to 9-lobed leaves, with oval, cut leaflets, to 2 in. (50 mm) long. Many gold, yellow, trumpet-shaped, fringed flowers, to 2 in. (50 mm) long, in clusters in autumn–spring, forming podlike fruit containing seeds, in summer.
Attracts: Hummingbirds with flowers, nectar.
Plant hardiness: Zones 7–11.
Site/Soil: Full–filtered sun. Damp, well-drained humus. Fertility: Rich. 6.0–7.0 pH. Salt tolerant.
Planting: Space 4–5 ft. (1.2–1.5 m) apart.
Care: Easy. Keep evenly moist. Fertilize monthly. Pinch, prune to control growth, shape. Propagate by cuttings, seed.
Features: Good choice for espalier, hedges, trellises. Pest and disease resistant.

Name: Grape. *Vitis* species. VITACEAE.
Description: Over 20 species of medium-growing, climbing, woody, deciduous shrubs or vines, to 20 ft. (6 m) long, with papery, shedding brown bark. Textured, light green, round, deeply cut, lobed, pointed leaves, to 6 in. (15 cm) wide, turning purple, red in autumn. Inconspicuous green flowers in spring, forming berrylike, pulpy, edible or inedible grapes in autumn.
Attracts: Birds with fruit.
Plant hardiness: Zones 5–9, depending on species.
Site/Soil: Full sun–partial shade. Damp–dry, well-drained, sandy soil. Fertility: Average. 6.5–7.5 pH.
Planting: Space 6–10 ft. (1.8–3 m) apart.
Care: Easy. Allow surface soil to dry between waterings. Fertilize annually in spring. Prune to control growth in winter. Propagate by cuttings, seed.
Features: Good choice for accents, containers, espalier. Pest and disease resistant.

Name: Honeysuckle. *Lonicera* species. CAPRIFOLIACEAE.
Description: More than 150 species, cultivars of upright or climbing, deciduous or evergreen shrubs or vines, 3–30 ft. (90–900 cm) tall. Shiny, green or blue green, leathery, oval leaves, 1–6 in. (25–150 mm) long, some turning bronze in autumn–winter. Many coral, pink, white, yellow, sometimes fragrant, 2-lipped, tubular flowers, ½–2 in. (12–50 mm) long, in spring–autumn, form black, purple, red berries in autumn.
Attracts: Birds, butterflies, hummingbirds with flowers, berries.
Plant hardiness: Zones 4–9.
Site/Soil: Full sun–partial shade. Damp, well-drained soil. Fertility: Rich–average. 6.5–7.5 pH.
Planting: Spacing varies by species.
Care: Easy. Allow surface soil to dry between waterings. Propagate by cuttings, layering, seed.
Features: Good choice for fences, ground cover, hedges, trellises, walls. Moderate–very invasive. Aphid susceptible.

Name: Trumpet Vine; Trumpet Creeper. *Campsis radicans.* BIGNONIACEAE.

Description: Fast-growing, semi-evergreen or deciduous vine, to 20 ft. (6 m) or longer, with clinging holdfasts. Textured, feathery, divided leaves, each with 9- to 11-toothed leaflets, 2½ in. (65 mm) long. Showy, orange, scarlet, trumpet-shaped, flaring flowers, 3 in. (75 mm) long, in large showy clusters, in summer, form seed-filled capsules, 5 in. (13 cm) long, in autumn.

Attracts: Birds, hummingbirds with flowers, nectar, seed.

Plant hardiness: Zones 5–10.

Site/Soil: Full sun–partial shade. Damp, well-drained, sandy soil. Fertility: Average. 6.5–7.0 pH.

Planting: Space according to use.

Care: Easy. Allow surface soil to dry between waterings. Fertilize monthly. Prune to control growth. Propagate by cuttings, layering, seed.

Features: Good choice for accents, fences, trellises, walls. Good for shade structures. Pest and disease resistant.

> **Warning**
>
> Foliage of trumpet vine may cause skin irritation in sensitive individuals. Wear gloves whenever you handle foliage parts.

Name: Virginia Creeper; Woodbine. *Parthenocissus quinquefolia.* VITACEAE.

Description: Fast-growing, spreading, deciduous vine to 50 ft. (15 m) or longer, with clinging holdfasts. Textured, bronze turning dark green, 5-lobed, deeply toothed leaves, to 6 in. (15 cm) long, turning purple, red in autumn. Inconspicuous greenish flowers, in early summer, form blue, black, round berries in autumn.

Attracts: Birds with berries.

Plant hardiness: Zones 3–10.

Site/Soil: Full sun–full shade. Moist, well-drained soil. Fertility: Rich–average. 6.5–7.0 pH.

Planting: Space according to use.

Care: Easy. Allow surface soil to dry between waterings. Avoid fertilizing. Prune to train, shape during growth. Propagate by cuttings, layering, seed.

Features: Good choice for accents, fences, trellises, walls. Good for shade structures. Japanese beetle, caterpillar, scale and leaf spot, mildew susceptible.

Name: Wisteria. *Wisteria* species. FABACEAE (LEGUMINOSAE).

Description: Several species of fast-growing, climbing, woody deciduous vines, to 100 ft. (30 m) or longer, lacking clinging holdfasts. Alternate, soft, green, feathery, divided leaves, each with up to 20 leaflets, to 3 in. (75 mm) long, turning yellow in autumn. Many blue, lilac, white, pealike flowers, to ¾ in. (19 mm) long, in showy, grapelike, dangling clusters, to 1 ft. (30 cm) long, in summer, forming dry, beanlike pods in autumn.

Attracts: Butterflies, hummingbirds with flowers, nectar, seed.

Plant hardiness: Tender. Zones 5–10.

Site/Soil: Full sun. Damp, well-drained soil. Fertility: Average–low. 6.0–7.0 pH.

Planting: Space according to use.

Care: Easy. Allow surface soil to dry between waterings. Avoid fertilizing. Pinch, prune to train, shape, control growth. Protect from frost. Provide sturdy supports. Propagate by cuttings, division, grafting, seed.

Features: Good choice for accents, fences, trellises, walls. Good for shade structures. Invasive, heavy. Pest and disease resistant.

USDA Plant Hardiness Around the World
North America

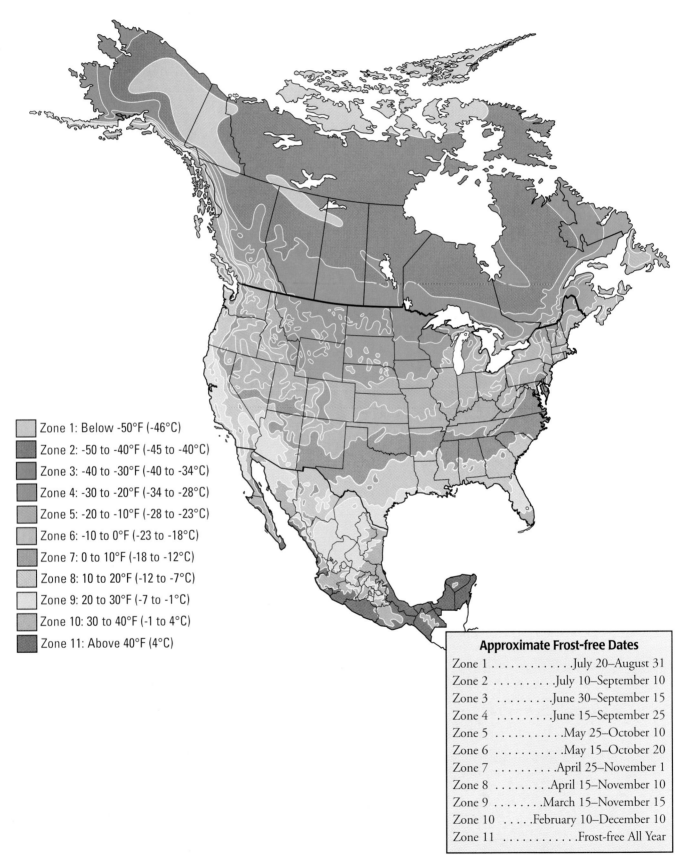

Zone 1: Below -50°F (-46°C)

Zone 2: -50 to -40°F (-45 to -40°C)

Zone 3: -40 to -30°F (-40 to -34°C)

Zone 4: -30 to -20°F (-34 to -28°C)

Zone 5: -20 to -10°F (-28 to -23°C)

Zone 6: -10 to 0°F (-23 to -18°C)

Zone 7: 0 to 10°F (-18 to -12°C)

Zone 8: 10 to 20°F (-12 to -7°C)

Zone 9: 20 to 30°F (-7 to -1°C)

Zone 10: 30 to 40°F (-1 to 4°C)

Zone 11: Above 40°F (4°C)

Approximate Frost-free Dates	
Zone 1	July 20–August 31
Zone 2	July 10–September 10
Zone 3	June 30–September 15
Zone 4	June 15–September 25
Zone 5	May 25–October 10
Zone 6	May 15–October 20
Zone 7	April 25–November 1
Zone 8	April 15–November 10
Zone 9	March 15–November 15
Zone 10	February 10–December 10
Zone 11	Frost-free All Year

USDA Plant Hardiness Around the World
Australia

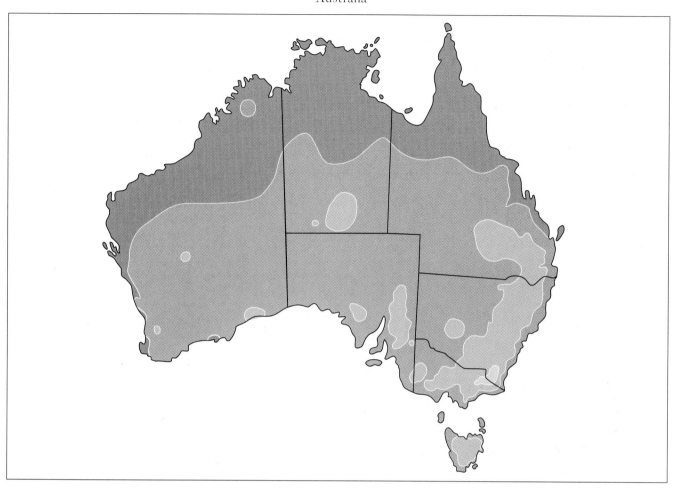

South Africa

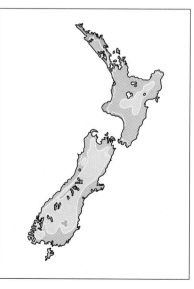

New Zealand

Europe

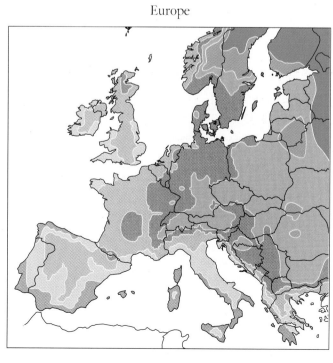

ON-LINE   INDEX

INDEX

D–E

Daisy, 97, 103
Dark-eyed Junco, 7
Deep-throated flowers, 76
Delphinium species, 102
Dianthus species, 104
Dictamnus albus, 19
Digitalis species, 101
Disease, natural treatment, 24
Doves, 18, 90
Downy Woodpecker, 18
Eastern Bluebird, 73
Echinacea purpurea, 98
Echinops species, 106
Elder, 109
Elderberry, 109
Eyed Brown Satyr butterfly, 61

F

Feeder 16, 18, 31, 34, 37, 75, 83
Fertilizers 51, 56–57
Field guides
  bird-watching, 93
  hummingbirds, 78
  songbirds, 86
Firethorn, 110
Florist's Geranium, 100
Flossflower, 100
Flowers
  attract birds, 19
  deep-throated, 76
  layered planting, 19
  nectar-producing, 19
  planting, 59
  succession creation, 47
Flyways, 88
Four-O'Clock, 100
Foxglove, 101
Fuchsia, 16, 110
Fuchsia × hybrids, 110

G

Gaillandia species, 97
Garden
  aromatic herb, 34
  butterfly, 15, 62
  care, 24, 44
  constituents to attract wildlife, 2, 13
  design of wildlife, 35
  features to attract birds/butterflies, 6
  flowers to attract birds, 19
  main features, 35
  natural, 10
  observation points, 36
  plan creation, 33
  planning flowchart, 28

planning pond, 41
  structures, 6, 36
  water, 8
  wildlife, 13
Garden Nasturtium, 104
Garden Snapdragon, 105
Geranium, Florist's, 100
GFCI. *See* Ground fault circuit interrupter (GFCI)
Gladiolus species, 101
Globe Thistle, 106
Gloriosa Daisy, 97
Goldenrod, 101
Goldfinch, 20, 40, 88
Gooseberry, 109
Grape, Oregon, 112
Grapes, 23, 46, 114
Grasses, 23
Ground cover, 23
Ground fault circuit interrupter (GFCI), 40

H

Hackberry, 21
Helianthus species, 106
Hemerocallis flava, 19
Hesperis matronalis, 19
Heuchera sanguinea, 99
Holly, 21, 110
Hollyhock, 64, 102
Honeysuckle, 19, 21, 46, 114
House finches, 17
Hummingbirds, 16
  Anna's, 74
  attracting, 74
  Costa's, 74
  Cuban Emerald, 16
  in Eastern U.S., 78
  field guide, 78
  insect food, 5
  nectar water, 74
  North American, 77
  Ruby-throated, 16, 20, 78
  Rufus, 16
  in Western U.S., 78
Humus, 42
Hybrid Fuchsia, 110
Hydrangea petiolaris, 23

I–J–K

Ilex species, 110
Indian Paintbrush, 103
Indian Pink, 98
Insects, natural control methods, 71
Irrigation, in-ground, 44
Jessamine, Night, 111
Junco, 2, 7

Juneberry, 112
Killdeer, 90
Kolkwitzia amabilis, 108

L

Lantana hybrids, 113
Larkspur, 102
Lavender, 105, 111
Lavendula species, 111
Lenicera species, 114
Lesser Goldfinch, 20
Lethe eurydice, 61
Lilac, 16, 21, 46, 111
Lily, Sword, 101
Limonium species, 105
Lobelia cardinalis, 98
Lonicera 'Alabama Crimson, 23
Lupine, 102
Lupinus species and hybrids, 102

M

Mahonia species, 112
Marigold, 103
Marvel-of-Peru, 100
Michaelmas Daisy, 103
Milkweed, 46, 64, 103
Mirabilis jalapa, 100
Monarch butterfly, 3, 62
Monarda didyma, 96
Mosaic virus, 71
Moths, 14, 62
Mountain Bluebirds, 17
Mountain Chickadees, 80
Mourning Dove, 18
Mulch, 44, 56, 58

N–O

Nasturtium, Garden, 104
Nectar 74–75
Nectar feeder, 16, 75
Nectar-producing flowers, 19
Nematodes, 71
Nesting baskets, 7
Night Jassamine, 111
North American flyway, 88
Nursery, butterfly, 65
Oregon Grape, 112
Oswego Tea, 96

P–Q

Paintbrush, Indian, 93
Parsley, 3
Parthenocissus species, 23, 115
Passiflora species, 23
Pelargonium species, 100
Penstemon species, 96

I N D E X